The Blood of Christ in the Theology of William Tyndale

Ralph S. Werrell

James Clarke & Co

James Clarke & Co
P.O. Box 60
Cambridge
CB1 2NT

www.jamesclarke.co
publishing@jamesclarke.co

ISBN: 978 0 227 17487 6

British Library Cataloguing in Publication Data
A record is available from the British Library

Contents

Preface

In 1955, I bought 42 volumes of the Parker Society works of the English Reformers. I found that my understanding of the Bible resonated with the theology of the earliest English Reformers. Before I was ordained in 1956, I decided that I would obtain my doctorate on some aspect of the theology of those early English Reformers. Because I felt that God wanted me to have a pastoral ministry covering 'all sorts and conditions of men', and which covered all ages, from the cradle to the grave, I realised that my doctorate would have to wait until after I retired.

As I approached retirement, I knew that I had to get my 'academic' brain working, and so, I started work on a Lambeth Diploma. I chose for my research the topic "Church and State in the theology of the Early English Reformation". William Tyndale, Hugh Latimer, Nicholas Ridley, John Bradford and John Hooper were chosen. Then I wondered if what I was doing was the best way for me to achieve my purpose. I felt that I was going to end up with a shallow doctrine of Church and State from five Reformers (otherwise I would need more words than I was allowed for my Lambeth Diploma). I asked my Supervisor, "Would it be better to only deal with one Reformer, and look at the doctrine in depth?" He, seeing how my mind was working, said, "It would be better. As you have done more work on William Tyndale than the others, you should concentrate on him." He then got this change in plan approved by the Archbishop's Theological Committee.

Shortly before I retired, I had a sabbatical so that I could plan the subject for my proposed doctorate. I knew that it had to be on a doctrine in Tyndale's theology. As I read the Parker Society's three volumes of the *Works of William Tyndale* for the fourth time, I was struck by the frequency with which the words "the blood of Christ" appeared in his writings. Further readings of Tyndale's Works made me realise that it was impossible to consider any single doctrine of Tyndale's until one understood the whole of his theology. So, my doctorate had to be "The Theology of William Tyndale".

The year 1994 was the year of my retirement; my wife and I were looking for a suitable place to live and wanted to make it ready for us to move. There was still the Parish to care for, and I also wanted to ensure that the early days following my retirement ran smoothly for the first three months of the interregnum. I hardly had any time to think further about my retirement task, even less about my doctorate when the Quincentenary of William Tyndale was announced. At the first "Oxford International Tyndale Conference" (September 1994), I presented a paper, "Tyndale and the blood of Christ". Before preparing this paper, I had extracted all the doctrinal references to the blood of Christ[1] in the three Parker Society volumes of Tyndale's Works. These, plus the references in the *1525, New Testament*, and in Tyndale's "Supplication to the King",[2] are the base texts for this present work.

To keep this book within reasonable bounds, it has been necessary to keep separate the blood of Christ in each doctrine or division, but also not draw Tyndale's doctrines into a coherent whole, for this would have doubled the length of this book. Also, I have not been able to use every reference under the relevant heading. As Tyndale's 1525 *New Testament* was not included in the Parker Society Works, I have modernised its spelling, and also, where necessary, capitalised proper names.

This book had to wait until I had written *The Theology of William Tyndale*, which is based on my doctoral dissertation, and *The Roots of William Tyndale's Theology*. The roots of Tyndale's theology, I had discovered in my research for my Lambeth Diploma, reached back to the English Wycliffites, and not to the Continental Reformers.

What will be obvious to the reader of this book is that the blood of Christ flows like a golden river through every aspect of Tyndale's theology, and the blood of Christ affects every aspect of man's salvation.

First, the importance of the blood of Christ is not just for man's new creation – faith and repentance leading man to his new birth as a child of God – but for God's elect children to fulfil every aspect of their Christian life. It became clear that the Holy Spirit must sprinkle the Christian life with the blood of Christ if one was going to be acceptable to God.

Christ's work was to restore creation to its pristine glory, and I have been asked, "If you are right, why do we say, 'Christ came for us men and our salvation?'" The answer is simple, although my illustration can only be an imaginative picture. My car has broken down, and I take it to the garage. The mechanic is only interested in the broken part. He repairs it, and the whole car is restored to its original condition. It was man, through Adam's disobedience to God's commandment, that caused the breakdown of God's creation.

---

1. This does not include references to 'the blood' in the sacrament, except where it has a theological meaning.
2. Foxe, *Acts and Monuments*, vol. 5, pt 1, p. 131.

Second, man's salvation is totally the work of God, with the Father electing those to be his children, the Son shedding his blood for the elect and the Holy Spirit working in applying the blood of Christ to enable the elect to fulfil every aspect of their life as a child of God. Although the Christian can do nothing without the Holy Spirit's enabling him through the blood of Christ, the child of God has a free will, with the ability to disobey as well as to obey God's will. In the same way as a child, in a loving family, wants to please his parents but sometimes does things that are wrong and wishes that he hadn't done so, a child of God, even if he would not sin deliberately, nevertheless, he does sin of frailty and regrets what he has done.

I apologise if there seems to be a repetition of what is written in my earlier books. These books view Tyndale's theology more from the point of separate doctrines of our Christian faith. This book examines one doctrine only – the doctrine that is the base for every doctrine that affects the whole of one's Christian life.

It is easy for us to separate our life into several compartments, as if we can isolate one from another. Books have been written on one aspect of our Christian life, as if it can be considered apart from the many other aspects of our life. There are books on Christian doctrine; on worship; on prayer; on spirituality and on the Christian's life.[1] But, the doctrine of the blood of Christ does away with all these divisions – it covers every part of our life, and there is nothing we think or do that does not depend on the Holy Spirit sprinkling Christ's blood on us, sanctifying our every thought and action, enabling us to grow and develop as children of our heavenly Father. In considering 'the blood of Christ' in relation to its place in other doctrines, I have sometimes stayed only with references to Christ's blood; but there are times when that makes that section jerky, and so I have smoothed it out with other references from Tyndale's writings.

When I discovered the importance of Christ's blood as I approached retirement, it revolutionised my theology. I wondered why I had not seen it as I read my Bible. I had always had some unanswered theological questions that did not seem to have a scriptural answer. Tyndale had found the scriptural answer to those questions in the blood of Christ.

Of course, there will always be some unanswered questions, although there are still those where Christians have sought to discover an answer. But is it right for Christians to seek an answer when God has not revealed, in the Bible, what we would like to know? The commonest hidden secret concerns predestination. Did God predestine those who were to be saved, or were any predestined to damnation (double predestination)? This is perhaps the most divisive question between different Christian theologies, but there are

---

1. This does not mean that these books are not important; they need to be written and read alongside the Scriptures.

others that divide the Church into different schemata or denominations. In his *Prologue to Romans*, Tyndale has the clearest statement for us regarding these questions where the scriptures do not give us a clear answer.

> But here must a mark be set to those unquiet, busy, and high-climbing spirits, how far they all go; which first of all bring hither their high reasons and pregnant wits, and begin first from an high to search the bottomless secrets of God's predestination, whether they be predestinate or not. . . . But follow thou the order of this epistle, and noosel thyself with Christ, and learn to understand what the law and the gospel mean.[1]

There are also other instances where Tyndale warns us not to try to probe God's secrets, where there is no answer to be found in the Bible because God has not revealed it to us.

> So was the scripture given us to guide us in our way and works ghostly. The way is Christ; and the promises in him are our salvation, if we long for them. Now if we shall leave that right use and turn ourselves unto vain questions, and to search the unsearchable secrets of God; then no doubt shall the scripture blind us, as it hath done our schoolmen and our subtle disputers.[2]

In conclusion, Tyndale writes in *Mammon*, "Let us therefore give diligence rather to do the will of God, than to search his secrets, which are not profitable for us to know."[3] In this book, there are no answers to God's secrets, but a revealing of God's open will through the writings of William Tyndale, who, I believe, was one of the great Reformation theologians.

When one reads Tyndale's writings, one is struck by his English. Although he was writing almost six hundred years ago, his writings are easy to read and understand. Furthermore, his every word counts, for he does not waste words, which means that if one tries to express Tyndale's meaning in one's own words, it would invariably be much longer and probably be less easy to understand.

Therefore, I have allowed Tyndale to speak for himself, rather than summarising what he has written, or trying to put his thoughts in my own words. My aim, in writing my books, is to be faithful to Tyndale, so that his understanding of the Scriptures may be clearly seen, and not my interpretation of his theology. Therefore, in some of my quotations I have followed Tyndale's advice regarding the scriptures that we might see the truth through "the circumstances, and what goeth before and after; that I may know whether thine interpretation be the right sense."[4]

---

1. William Tyndale, *Romans, PS-1*, p. 505.
2. William Tyndale, *Obedience, PS-1*, p. 317.
3. William Tyndale, *Mammon, PS-1*, p. 89.
4. William Tyndale, *Obedience, PS-1*, p. 147.

1. Introduction

That their spirit reign above their flesh, leading it to virtues, and not the flesh above the spirit, leading it to vices. And that Christ spend not in vain his precious blood on us.   Psalm 20:2
(Two Revisions of Rolle's English Psalter Commentary, vol 1.
(EETS O.S. 340), p. 255)

"The meaning of the word 'blood' in Scripture is obviously of great importance to all Christian students of the Bible, because of its frequent use in connection with Christ Himself and with the Christian doctrine of salvation."[1] These are the opening words of Alan Stibbs's monograph, *The Meaning of the Word 'Blood' in Scripture.* Although it is dated the second updated edition being published in 1954, much of what he writes about academia's view of the biblical use of 'blood' still holds true. Alan Stibbs's explanation of the scriptural meaning of blood is, I believe, relevant today. And in this book we will be considering Tyndale's understanding of the blood of Christ as it affects our relationship with God and the whole of our Christian life.

Alan Stibbs continues:

> What we need ultimately to discover, and to be sure of, is the theological significance of the word 'blood' in its use in the New Testament with reference to the sacrifice of Christ. This is the more important because in this connection the word is used so often. As Vincent Taylor has pointed out, the 'blood' of Christ is mentioned in the writings of the New Testament nearly three times as often as 'the Cross' of Christ, and five times as frequently as the 'death' of Christ. The term 'blood' is, in fact, a chief method of reference to the sacrifice of Christ, particularly in contexts which define its efficacy.[2]

Stibbs wrote of our need to discover "the theological significance of the word 'blood" in the New Testament". I am certain he would have agreed

---

1. A.M. Stibbs, *The Meaning of the Word 'Blood' in Scripture*, p. 3.
2. Ibid. (See Vincent Taylor, *The Atonement in N.T. Teaching*, 1945).

with Tyndale about the importance of 'the blood of Christ' as he made the theological link between the sacrificial blood in the Old Testament with Christ's blood in the New.

There are many positive references in the New Testament, linking it to the sacrifices in the Old Testament, especially in *The Epistle to the Hebrews*, that teach us much of what we need to know about our Christian faith. The context in which we are told, "Jesus Christ is the same yesterday and today, and for ever" (Heb. 13:8), links the Old Testament sacrifices for sin with Christ's sacrifice for sin – for the "yesterday" refers back in time to the Mosaic sacrifices; "today" refers to the time of the Christian Church, from Christ's sacrifice on the Cross; whilst "for ever" is to be understood that Jesus Christ will be with us throughout all eternity. For unlike most Christian theologies, Tyndale did not consider that there is a complete break between the Old and the New Testaments. He believed that there is a continuity between the two periods. God has not changed; he is the God who drove Adam out of the Garden of Eden and the same One who chose Abraham and promised him that he would have many descendants. He is the same God who told Abraham to sacrifice his only son, who, when Isaac was going to be sacrificed, provided a lamb to take Isaac's place. He is the God who provided the Israelites sacrificial lambs for their sins. He is the same One who gave Jesus Christ, his only Son, to be a sacrifice for our sins, for he is "The Lamb of God, which taketh away the sin of the world" (Jn 1:29). He is the same God who gave the Israelites the Passover Lamb, and who gave us his Son, for "Christ our passover is sacrificed for us" (1 Cor. 5:7). So, He is the same for ever to those "whose names are written in the book of life of the Lamb slain from the foundation of the world" (Rev. 13:8). Tyndale understood that 'yesterday's' blood in the Old Testament sacrifices pointed forward to 'today', when we look back to the time Christ sacrificed his blood for us on the Cross at Calvary.

It is obvious that Tyndale realised the importance of those facts, for one does not have to read far into Tyndale's writings to realise the importance of the 'blood of Christ' in his theology. Whatever doctrine we choose to consider, we find that it depends on the blood of Christ if we are to understand it. Yet, often academics believe that Tyndale's theology of Christ's blood is the same as Luther's theology of the Cross, even though the Cross is relevant to only a few doctrines. The error of that belief will be made clear as we examine Tyndale's theology of Christ's blood. Although there are a few instances where Tyndale's mention of 'blood' could be replaced by 'cross', the vast majority of these are where 'cross' would not make any sense. From the number of times Tyndale refers to verses from *The Epistle to the Hebrews*, it is obvious that the link between that Epistle and the Old

Testament sacrifices was important for Tyndale's theology of the blood of Christ. The covenant of salvation that God made with his chosen people is sealed with Christ's blood; in fact, Tyndale's theology is summarised at the end of *The Epistle to the Hebrews*.

> Now the God of peace, who brought again from the dead the great Shepherd of the sheep with the blood of the eternal covenant, even our Lord Jesus, make you perfect in every good thing to do his will, working in us that which is well-pleasing in his sight, through Jesus Christ; to whom be the glory for ever and ever. Amen (Heb. 13:20, 21).

Hebrews clearly links the blood in the Old Testament sacrifices to Christ's sacrificial blood shed on the Cross in fulfilment of the 'eternal covenant'.

> Moses offered half the blood to God, and sprinkled the people with the other half, to confirm the covenant and to bind both parties: neither was there any covenant made that was not confirmed with blood, as it is rehearsed in Hebrews ix.; and as we see in the books of Moses, whose custom of blood-shedding was not only to confirm those old covenants, but also to be a prophecy of the blood that should be shed to confirm this testament.[1]

To those who insist that Tyndale's theology, following the teaching of the scriptures, of Christ's blood is the same as Luther's theology of the Cross, I ask them to replace 'blood' with 'cross' in Hebrews 9:11-22, especially, "all things are cleansed with blood, and apart from shedding of blood there is no remission". Yet, it is clear that this refers to Christ's sacrifice on the Cross.

As we are only considering one doctrine – even though 'the blood of Christ' relates to every part of Tyndale's theology – there will be a certain amount of overlap, and I will, in places, refer to a passage that has already been quoted, rather than quoting it again. In many of the chapters, we will find an incomplete explanation of Tyndale's theology, but only the importance of Christ's blood in that doctrine. Unfortunately, this can give us a sense of 'incompleteness', and I can only refer you to my earlier books.[2] I consider that by looking at different aspects of a single doctrine, we are following the line of a concentric spiral. No part of the spiral is completely separate from any other part, but there are times when several aspects of the doctrine appear closer vertically between different rings in the spiral than to those aspects we considered

---

1. William Tyndale, *Sacraments, PS-1*, p. 363f.
2. R.S. Werrell, *The Theology of William Tyndale* (2006) and *The Roots of William Tyndale's Theology* (2013).

just before or after it. Frequently, we find that when Tyndale mentions 'the blood of Christ', apart from its referring to our main doctrine, he draws our attention to other related doctrines. For Tyndale is not writing a theological handbook, but about the Christian's life as a child of God. When Tyndale mentions the blood of Christ, he often refers to more than one doctrine. Where possible I have tried not to repeat the same quotation in a different context.

We must remember that Tyndale used different words for covenant, but his covenantal theology remained the same from 1525 to 1536. Clebsch attempted to fit Tyndale's theology into some preconceived theological *schemata*, and regarding the change Tyndale made of testament to covenant, Clebsch wrote, "Although any continuous narrative of Tyndale's career from 1532 until its end in 1536 builds on supposition after supposition, his theology, newly organized around the idea of covenant as a bipartite, divine-human contract binding upon both parties, shouts itself from every writing attributable to the period."[1] Clebsch believed that Tyndale wrote 'testament' in his early writings; then his theology changed to a more Reformed theology, and so we find 'covenant' in his later writings. Tyndale realised that his readers might get confused by this change. So, in his writings that bridged the time he made that change, he wrote that 'testament' and 'covenant' meant the same. But Clebsch totally ignored this point. Tyndale wrote, "God . . . hath made a testament or covenant, and hath bound himself, and hath sealed his obligation with Christ's blood." Again, "to testify and confirm the testament or covenant made in Christ's blood and body."[2]

Clebsch believed that Tyndale's *Prologue to Romans* (1526) was a translation of Luther's *Preface to Romans*; therefore, Tyndale's theology between 1525 and 1530 was Lutheran. Yet, I have been unable to find where, during those years, Tyndale's theology disagreed with his later writings, which Clebsch says were not Lutheran. Clebsch's theory basically depended on Tyndale's use of some of Luther's writings. He took those early writings where Tyndale used Luther as a base text for what he wanted to write, without considering why, so often, Tyndale kept breaking off from his good translation, changing or deleting Luther's words and inserting his own. These changes altered Luther's theology. There are also many places where Tyndale inserted theological material of his own, where Luther thought it unnecessary.[3]

Leonard Trinterud analysed Luther's *Preface* and Tyndale's *Prologue*

---

1. W.A. Clebsch, *England's Earliest Protestants*, p. 181.
2. William Tyndale, *Obedience, PS-1*, p. 292; *Sacraments, PS-1*, p. 381, et al.
3. Ralph S. Werrell, "Tyndale's Disagreement with Luther in the Prologue to the Epistle to the Romans".

to Romans and concluded that one eighth of Tyndale's was a good translation of half of Luther's. I have been surprised at the way in which Clebsch's work was accepted as accurate, as he had not taken the findings of Trinterud into account.[1] Also, the academic reluctance to accept the findings of Paul Lauchlin, who started his doctoral research to prove Clebsch was right in his theory, and ended up being forced to state that Clebsch had not understood Tyndale's theology and therefore had stated as fact what was untrue.[2]

There are two covenants that are important in Tyndale's theology. First, there is 'The Covenant', made between the Persons of the Trinity, as God the Father, who elects those he shall save from fallen mankind; as God the Son, who became man and shed his blood for man's salvation; and as God the Holy Spirit, who sprinkles the blood of Christ on those being saved, enabling them to become children of God.[3] Second, there is the 'General Covenant', made between God and man, effecting man's salvation. This covenant is multiple, for, as Tyndale wrote, where we find God making a promise to us, there is a covenant. "Wherefore I have ever noted the covenants in the margins, and also the promises. Moreover, where thou findest a promise, and no covenant expressed therewith, there must thou understand a covenant."[4] Tyndale was determined to help those who read the Word of God:

> I thought it my duty, most dear reader, to warn thee before, and to shew thee the right way in, and to give thee the true key to open it withal, and to arm thee against false prophets and malicious hypocrites; whose perpetual study is to blind the scripture with glosses, and there to lock it up where it should save the soul, and to make us shoot at a wrong mark, to put our trust in those things that profit their bellies only, and slay our souls.[5]

In Chapter 2, we consider the covenant between the Persons of the Trinity. We begin our consideration of the blood of Christ where man's salvation seems to have a secondary place: "He chose us in him before the foundation of the world" (Eph. 1:4). So, we start with the covenant made between the Persons of the Trinity, as it applies to us from before the beginning of the world to its end – for God knew what was going to happen after he had

---

1. L.J. Trinterud, "A Reappraisal of William Tyndale's Debt to Martin Luther".
2. Paul Laughlin, "The Brightness of Moses Face".
3. Tyndale does not spell out this covenant, but there are passages in his writings that link the work of the three Persons of the Trinity in a way that can only be understood as covenantal: see, *Answer, PS-3*, p. 111f.
4. William Tyndale, *Prologue Matthew, PS-1*, p. 471.
5. Ibid., p. 469.

created the earth. God knew how Satan was going to tempt man and that man would fall to the Devil's temptation. God also knew how he was going to break Satan's hold on man and the worlds, destroy the Devil and restore man and his creation to its original state.

In Chapter 3, we pass from Satan's temptation of Adam and Eve to man's Fall and to man dying spiritually to God. Man was then cast out of the Garden of Eden, but God started his work of restoring man and breaking Satan's power. We then follow the early stages of man's salvation, and the way by which God revealed his final purpose, by signs revealing how man would finally be set free from his slavery to sin. We trace the progress from Adam's Fall which led to man's slavery to the Devil's power; to God's plan to set man free from his bondage to the Devil. God made a promise to Abraham that one of his descendants would liberate man from that slavery. The history of the Israelites illustrated this. They became slaves to Pharaoh, and, through God's call to Moses, the blood of the sacrificial lamb liberated them from their slavery so that they became the children of God. It was through Christ's blood, portrayed by the blood of the Passover lamb, that the Israelites were freed from Pharaoh's power. In the same way, Christians are freed by Christ's blood from bondage to our Pharaoh, the Devil's power. For the blood of the Passover and the blood of the sacrifices were, figuratively, Christ's blood that would be shed when God the Son shed his blood in fulfilment of his part in the Trinitarian Covenant. This enabled man to be created anew and become a child of God the Father.

In Chapter 4, we are concerned with the world, that had been destroyed by Adam's sin, being re-created. God fulfils his plans for his new World. Fallen man who is "dead in trespasses and sins" (Eph. 2:1) becomes a new creation in every aspect of his Christian's life through the Holy Spirit sprinkling the blood of Christ on him.

Chapter 5 brings us to the life of a child of God, to the worship of the Christian Church and to the place of the Sacraments for the Christian community. The continuity of God's purpose from the Old Testament to the New Testament becomes clear to us from our study of Tyndale's opening of the Scriptures and his explanation of its unity, for in both Testaments the blood has the same power for man's salvation.

Chapter 6 considers the different ways in which the Church has erred in its understanding of the blood of Christ and the way in which the Church has introduced various traditions that are not found in scripture, which are the result of the teaching of the pope's Church.

Chapter 7 sums up what we have discovered of the importance of the 'blood of Christ' in Tyndale's theology.

We then, finally, have the Appendices, detailing the use of Christ's blood in Tyndale's writings. The Appendices will draw to our attention some important references to 'the blood of Christ' that were omitted in the main text to ensure that the text was not overloaded. Often, these will only be references of where they may be found in Tyndale's writings.

We will see that the blood of Christ, in Tyndale's writings, covers every theological doctrine: from man's election "before the foundation of the world" (Eph. 1:4), through God's dealing with man through the Old and New Testaments, even to the end of time; for "apart from shedding of blood there is no remission" (Heb. 9:22) of sin.

2. The Trinity, Election and the Covenant

It is impossible to separate the blood of Christ from the doctrine of man and his salvation, but in this chapter, I have taken some instances where there is to be a greater emphasis on the Persons of the Trinity, and God as the author of man's salvation. When man sinned and was cast out of the Garden of Eden, God had not written him off; he was still part of God's plan for his creation. God's covenant was to restore man and his creation and, at the same time, to destroy Satan and all the power that he had gained through man's disobedience.

> Christ, which is contrary to the devil, came to destroy the works of the devil in us, and to give us a new birth, a new nature, and to sow new seed in us, that we should, by the reason of that birth, sin no more. For the seed of that birth, that is to wete the Spirit of God and the lively seed of his word sown in our hearts, keepeth our hearts that we cannot consent to sin; as the seed of the devil holdeth the hearts of his, that they cannot consent to good.[1]

The Trinity

We catch a glimpse of the Trinity's place in Tyndale's doctrine at the end of his *Prologue to the Prophet Jonas*. Tyndale states that there is nothing that we can do for our salvation

> but receive only of his mercy with our repenting faith, through Jesus Christ our Lord and only Saviour: unto whom, and unto God our Father through him, and unto his Holy Spirit, that only purgeth, sanctifieth, and washeth us in the innocent blood of our redemption, be praise for ever. Amen.[2]

In this quotation, we see how the Three Persons of the Trinity work together for man's salvation, and also the different part each Person has in the restoration of creation, and the enabling of man to be born anew.

1. William Tyndale, *Exposition 1 John, PS-2*, p. 190.
2. William Tyndale, *Prologue to the Prophet Jonas, PS-1*, p. 466.

We find Tyndale explaining the salvific work of the Persons of the Trinity, that the Son became a man in order to shed his blood and to overcome the power that Satan gained through Adam's disobedience to God. Christ's sacrificial blood restored man to life and enabled the Father to be man's heavenly Father. The blood of Christ also opens the way for the Holy Spirit to do his work of sanctifying God's elect. In his *Preface* to his *1525 New Testament*, Tyndale summarised this work of the Trinity for the restoration of God's creation:

> In Christ God loved us, his elect and chosen, before the world began, and reserved us unto the knowledge of his Son and of his holy gospel; and when the gospel is preached to us, he openeth our hearts, and giveth us grace to believe, and putteth the Spirit of Christ in us; and we know him as our Father most merciful, and consent to the law, and love it inwardly in our heart, and sorrow because we cannot: which will (sin we of frailty never so much) is sufficient, till more strength be given us; the blood of Christ hath made satisfaction for the rest.[1]

Tyndale clearly believed that our salvation is the combined work of the Trinity, when he wrote, "Faith in Christ's blood, and in the Father through him, is God's service in the Spirit."[2] But in some instances, the text is not clear on whether it is referring to the Trinity or to the work of one or more Persons of the Godhead, where it could mean 'the Father' or 'the Trinity' (e.g. "I am coupled to God by Christ's blood.").[3]

God the Father

God the Father has made a covenant with his chosen people, and nothing can break or supersede this covenant.

> If it were possible that all the angels of heaven could be mine enemies, yet would I hold me by the testament that my merciful and true Father hath made me in the blood of my Saviour, and so come unto all that is promised me, and Christ hath purchased for me, and give not a straw for them all.[4]

For there is nothing that can break God's promise to his chosen people; therefore, they are to comfort "their souls with the promises of their heavenly Father, confirmed with the blood of their Lord Christ".[5]

It is the Father's love that is so important for the Christian in his life,

---

1. William Tyndale, *1525, New Testament*, p. 7: also, *Pathway, PS-1*, p. 14f.
2. William Tyndale, *The Sacraments, PS-1*, p. 374.
3. William Tyndale, *1525, New Testament*, p. 14: also, *Pathway, PS-1*, p. 22.
4. William Tyndale, *Answer, PS-3*, p. 89 (see also fn. 43).
5. William Tyndale, *Exposition Matthew, PS-2*, p.17.

and Tyndale's theology depends largely on the loving relationship between God the Father and the Christian as a child in God's family. Christ's blood "obtained that God should love us first, and be our Father, and that a merciful Father".[1] We catch a glimpse of the greatness of God's love to us for, "A Christian man perceiveth that God is his Father, and loveth him even as he loved Christ when he shed his blood on the cross."[2]

In his *Exposition of the First Epistle of St John*, Tyndale argued against those who believe that we have to pray to God through the saints if we want our prayers answered.

> Why goest thou not unto thy father thine ownself? 'I am a sinner,' will they say, 'and dare not.' If thou go in the right way, thou hast no sin. Christ hath taken all thy sins from thee; and God hath no rod in his hand, nor looketh sour, but merrily, that it is a lust to behold his cheerful countenance, and offereth thee his hand.[3]

God the Son

The sacrifices in the Old Testament pointed to the day when Christ, the Son of God, would be sacrificed on the Cross, thus ending the need for any sacrificial blood to be shed. Now, God's people look back to Christ's blood being shed for their forgiveness and salvation.

> We be now in the day-light, and all the secrets of God, and all his counsel and will is opened unto us; and he that was promised should come and bless us, is come already, and hath shed his blood for us, and hath blessed us with all manner blessings, and hath obtained all grace for us, and in him we have all. Wherefore God henceforth will receive no more sacrifices of beasts of us, as thou readest, Heb. x.[4]

It is through Christ's blood that the door is opened for us into a relationship with God. For Christ's blood opened the way for us to know God as our loving Father, who, through the blood of Christ, restored to fallen mankind God the Holy Spirit.

"Christ himself, with all that he is or can do, is ours. His blood shedding and all that he did, doeth me as good service, as though I myself had done it."[5] Earlier, Tyndale had expanded this idea: "The blood of Christ hath obtained all things for us of God. Christ is our satisfaction, redeemer, deliverer, saviour from vengeance and wrath."[6]

---

1. William Tyndale, *1525, New Testament*, p. 10; *Pathway, PS-1*, p. 18f.
2. William Tyndale, *Pathway, PS-1*, p. 22.
3. William Tyndale, *Exposition 1 John, PS-2*, p. 168.
4. William Tyndale, *Prologue Numbers, PS-1*, p. 433.
5. William Tyndale, *1525, New Testament*, p. 11; *Pathway, PS-1*, p. 19.
6. William Tyndale, *Pathway, PS-1*, p. 15.

One of the clearest statements about Christ's work for man's salvation is found in his *Supplication to the King.*

> For Christ died for sinners, and is their Saviour, and his blood is their treasure, to pay for their sins. He is that fatted calf which was slain to make them good cheer withal, if they will repent and come to their Father again; and his merits are the goodly raiment to cover the naked deformities of their sins.[1]

The elect, unlike those of the papal Church, do not trust in the outward acts and ceremonies of the Church for their salvation. "Their hope of forgiveness is in Christ only; through his blood, and not in ceremonies."[2] Therefore, for anyone who is a Christian, "If he believe in Christ, then is he a member of Christ, Christ's brother, Christ's flesh, Christ's blood, Christ's spouse, coheir with Christ, and hath his Spirit in earnest, and is also spiritual."[3]

The reality of our Christian faith is revealed when the Holy Spirit enables us to love our neighbour as we love ourselves, and for us to reflect in our lives something of God's mercy to those around us, especially to those who are unable to repay us for our love for them. When we love our neighbour, we reveal that the blood of Christ has restored us to life and fellowship with God,

> we be merciful to the poor, for conscience to God, and of compassion and hearty love, which compassion and love spring of the love we have to God in Christ, for the pure mercy and love that he hath shewed on us: then have we a sure token that we are beloved of God, and washed in Christ's blood, and elect, by Christ's deserving, unto eternal life.[4]

Most of the references to God the Son that we are able to consider in the doctrine of 'the blood of Christ' relate to what Christ has done for us, rather than to his Person. They relate to the greatest work that Christ did – the shedding of blood for the salvation of man, the restoration of creation and the final defeat of the Devil.

God the Holy Spirit

The Holy Spirit is active in man's salvation; he applies the blood of Christ to God's elect, enabling them to be children of God the Father. God's

---

1. William Tyndale, *Supplication to the King, Nobles and Subjects of England, A & M, vol 5*, p. 131.
2. William Tyndale, *Answer, PS-3*, p. 114.
3. William Tyndale, *Obedience, PS-1*, p. 240.
4. William Tyndale, *Mammon, PS-1*, p. 107.

command to us is: "Love the Lord God with all thy heart, with all thy soul, and with all thy strength, and with all thy mind; and thy neighbour as thyself" (Lk. 10). Tyndale explains that we are amongst those chosen by God when we yearn to love our neighbour as ourself, and

> thou feelest lust thereunto, and thy spirit sigheth, mourneth, and longeth after strength to do it, take a sign and evident token thereby, that the Spirit of life is in thee, and that thou art elect to life everlasting by Christ's blood, whose gift and purchase is thy faith, and that Spirit that worketh the will of God in thee; whose gift also are thy deeds, or rather the deeds of the Spirit of Christ, and not thine.[1]

Jesus spoke to his disciples about the Holy Spirit and called him the Comforter. A Christian needs the comfort that the Holy Spirit can give him in his life, as he seeks to fulfil his life of faith and to witness God's love. For the Christian, "except he had felt the infinite mercy, goodness, love, and kindness of God, and the fellowship of the blood of Christ, and the comfort of the Spirit of Christ in his heart, he could never have forsaken anything for God's sake."[2]

For the Christian is aware of the power of God's law and the pull of sin in his life, but also of the power of God's Holy Spirit to strengthen, comfort and support him. "In the gospel, when we believe the promises, we receive the Spirit of life, and are justified in the blood of Christ from all things whereof the law condemned us."[3] There are many signs by which we know the Spirit of God works in us, proving to us that we are the Father's children. "Since I am coupled to God by Christ's blood, do I well, not for heaven's sake; but because I am heir of heaven by grace and Christ's purchasing, and have the Spirit of God, I do good freely for so is my nature."[4] However, Tyndale did not believe that our good works had any effect on our salvation, but that they only showed we were God's children. "Not that our works make us the sons of God, but testify only, and certify our consciense, that we are the sons of God; and that God hath chosen us, and washed us in Christ's blood; and hath put his Spirit in us."[5] For there is only one reason why our works are good and pleasing in God's sight, for "Christ's Spirit is poured into us, to bring forth good works, and our works are the fruits of the Spirit; and the kingdom is the deserving of Christ's blood; and so is faith, and the Spirit, and good works also."[6]

---

1. Ibid., p. 85.
2. Ibid., p. 109.
3. William Tyndale, *1525, New Testament*, p. 4.
4. Ibid., p. 14.
5. William Tyndale, *Mammon, PS-1*, p. 72.
6. Ibid., p. 83.

Although there are many instances where Tyndale shows that our faith is a gift given to us by God, he does not link it to the blood of Christ, although he frequently shows how everything of substance depends on the blood of Christ.

> But right faith is a thing wrought be the Holy Ghost in us, which changeth us, turneth us into a new nature, and begetteth us anew in God, and maketh us the sons of God, as thou readest in the first of John; and killeth the old Adam, and maketh us altogether new in the heart, mind, will, lust, and in all our affections and powers of the soul; the Holy Ghost ever accompanying her, and ruling the heart.[1]

We now pass onto the work of the Holy Spirit in the life of God's chosen people, and we start with our baptism. Tyndale says that the meaning of a sacrament is that it teaches us God's love and purpose for our Christian life. "So now if baptism preach me the washing in Christ's blood, so doth the Holy Ghost accompany it; and that deed of preaching through faith doth put away my sins."[2] They are children of God because "Christ hath anointed them with his Spirit and with his blood".[3] It is then that they are enabled to know and keep God's law, not in their own strength but through the power of the Holy Spirit. "Wherefore of a man's own strength is the law never fulfilled; we must have thereunto God's favour, and his Spirit, purchased by Christ's blood."[4] Neither do our good works have any value to earn us a place in God's kingdom, for our good works are "outward signs and outward fruits of faith and of the Spirit; which justify not a man, but shew that a man is justified already before God, inwardly in the heart, through faith, and through the Spirit purchased by Christ's blood."[5]

One of the ways by which the Holy Spirit works is through the preaching of God's word by godly preachers, for

> When a true preacher preacheth, the Spirit entereth the heart of the elect, and maketh them feel the righteousness of the law of God, and by the law the poison of their corrupt nature; and thence leadeth them, through repentance, unto the mercy that is in Christ's blood; and as an ointment healeth the body, even so the Spirit, through confidence and trust in Christ's blood, healeth the soul, and maketh her love the law of God.[6]

---

1. William Tyndale, *Prologue, Romans, PS-1*, p. 493.
2. William Tyndale, *Prologue, Leviticus, PS-1*, p. 424.
3. William Tyndale, *Answer, PS-3*, p. 179.
4. William Tyndale, *Prologue, Romans, PS-1*, p. 503.
5. Ibid., p. 497.
6. William Tyndale, *Exposition 1 John, PS-2*, p. 183f.

Then, the Holy Spirit protects the Christian, and in time of temptation, he stops him from drifting away from the profession of his baptism: "For the Spirit of God is in his heart, and comforteth him, and holdeth him fast to the rock of the merits of Christ's blood, in whom he is elect."[1]

Election

Before God created anything, he knew everything that was going to happen in the world he planned to make. He knew that man, to whom he would give charge to care for the world he had created, would succumb to Satan's temptations and allow sin to separate man from God. When that happened, as far as God was concerned, man would be spiritually dead.

In order to save man, God planned man's salvation and the total defeat of Satan and God's enemies through the blood of Christ. As we have seen, God made a covenant by which God the Father would elect, from fallen mankind, those who were to be his children; God the Son would shed his blood, to pay man's debt to the Trinity; and God the Holy Spirit would sprinkle the elect with that blood to cleanse them from their sin. Tyndale, quoting Ephesians 1:4, demonstrates that our Christian life depends entirely on God and that our good works follow:

> "He loved us in his beloved, by whom we have," saith Paul, "redemption through his blood, and forgiveness of sins." The forgiveness of sins, then, is our redemption in Christ, and not the reward of works. "In whom," saith he in the same place, "he chose us before the making of the world," that is, long before we did good works.[2]

Tyndale teaches us that our salvation depends on the power and working of God not only before the world was created but also today. He wrote, "Seeing the faith of the testament in Christ's blood is the life of the righteous, from the beginning of the world to the end."[3] After writing about the child's dependence on his father's love, Tyndale explains:

> Even so goeth it with God's elect. God chooseth them first, and they not God; as thou readest, John xv. And then he sendeth forth and calleth them, and sheweth them his good will, which he beareth unto them, and maketh them see both their own damnation in the law, and also the mercy that is laid up for them in Christ's blood, and thereto what he will have them do.[4]

1. William Tyndale, *Mammon, PS-1*, p. 78.
2. Ibid., p. 110f.
3. William Tyndale, *Sacraments, PS-1*, p. 374.
4. William Tyndale, *Answer, PS-3*, p. 35.

We can see the way in which this covenant works, between the Persons of the Trinity, for man's salvation; man plays no part in this process but is passive. Tyndale quotes, Matthew 6, "Take heed to your alms, that ye do it not in the sight of men, to the intent that you would be seen of them." "This putteth us in remembrance of our duty, and sheweth what followeth good works; not that works deserve it, but that the reward is laid up for us in store, and we thereunto elect, through Christ's blood, which the works testify."[1] Therefore, our works have an importance, for through them, we can know that we are elect, but our good works cannot be restricted, because we are following the example that God has given us.

> And Paul saith, "Counterfeit Christ." And Peter saith, "Christ died for you, and left you an example to follow his steps." Whatsoever therefore faith hath received of God through Christ's blood and deserving, that same must love shed out, every whit, and bestow it on our neighbours unto their profit, yea, and that though they be our enemies. What faith receiveth of God through Christ's blood, that must we bestow on our neighbours, though they be our enemies.[2]

When we feel the deep working of God in our life, Tyndale tells us to

> counterfeit and follow God in well-doing, then no doubt it is a sign that the Spirit of God is in you, and also the favour of God, which is not in the world; and that ye are inheritors of all the promises of God, and elect unto the fellowship of the blood of Christ.[3]

The fact that the Christian is chosen by God does not make his life easy, because his life is a constant fight against the Devil who seeks to reassert his power over the Christian and make him sin.

> The elect, having the law written in their breasts, and loving it in their spirits, sin there never; but without, in the flesh. Against which sin they fight continually, and minish it daily with the help of the Spirit, through prayer, fasting, and serving their neighbours lovingly with all manner service, out of the law that is written in their hearts. And their hope of forgiveness is in Christ only; through his blood, and not in ceremonies.[4]

The Covenant between God and Man

Although God has chosen those who will become his children, the fact that we are elect does not enable us to become God's children. There is

---

1. William Tyndale, *Mammon, PS-1*, p. 73.
2. William Tyndale, *Pathway, PS-1*, p. 20.
3. William Tyndale, *Mammon, PS-1*, p. 72.
4. William Tyndale, *Answer, PS-3*, p. 114.

another covenant, one between God and man, and it is with this covenant, we are concerned. As we saw in the Covenant between the Persons of the Trinity, Tyndale also used different words to express this covenant. In his early writings, Tyndale used 'testament', but in his later writings, he used 'covenant'. But in his writings at the beginning of that change of word, he wrote, 'covenant that is testament', or the other way round. Another word Tyndale used for covenant was 'appointment'. This covenant is that God will be our God, and we will be his people, and how we obtain this sonship. Although this is generally true, there are times when we find that Tyndale has used 'covenant', 'testament', or 'appointment' in his writings where we would not have expected to have found any of these words used.

For us to understand this covenant that God has made with his elect, we have to start with God, because until he has brought us to life, we are powerless to do anything, being spiritually dead.

> For first, God, which alone hath power to help or hurt, hath made appointment betwixt him and us, in Christ's blood; and hath bound himself to give us whatsoever we ask in his name, testifying thereto that there is no other name to be saved by; and that he will be a father unto us, and save us both in this life and in the life to come.[1]

If we are to know and understand this covenant that God has made with us, we must know and understand the scriptures, for

> all the good promises which are made us throughout all the scripture, for Christ's sake, for his love, his passion or suffering, his blood-shedding or death, are all made us on this condition or covenant on our party, that we henceforth love the law of God, to walk therein.[2]

And again, Tyndale wrote that the covenant between the Persons of the Trinity binds God to save his elect:

> God hath also made us promises, and hath sworn; yea, hath made a testament or a covenant, and hath bound himself, and hath sealed his obligation with Christ's blood, and confirmed it with miracles.[3]

Tyndale's doctrine of the covenant starts with God's call of Abraham, and he shows that this is the same covenant that exists between God and the Christian.

> The covenant, made between God and Abraham, saved the man-child as soon as it was born, yea, as soon as it had life in the mother's womb:

---

1. William Tyndale, *Exposition 1 John, PS-2*, p. 166.

2. William Tyndale, *Exposition Matthew, PS-2*, p. 6.

3. William Tyndale, *Obedience, PS-1*, p. 292.

for the covenant, that God would be God of Abraham's seed, went over the fruit as soon as it had life.

Tyndale then stated that the covenant applied to male and female children:

for as the covenant made to the faith of Abraham went over his seed as soon as it had life, and before the sign was put on them; even so must needs the covenant, made to all that believe in Christ's blood, go over that seed as soon as it hath life in the mother's womb, before the sign be put on it.[1]

This is followed by the Children of Israel, after they were freed from slavery under Pharaoh, with their journey through the wilderness. God taught Moses his covenant and his laws, and the meaning of the sacrifices the Israelites were to offer to God. Tyndale also explained the laws that God gave Moses for the Children of Israel and how they taught the Israelites the way of life that eventually would be fulfilled and replaced when Christ died on the Cross.

Part of his laws are ceremonies, that is to say, signs that put men in remembrance either of the benefits of God done already, as the Easter lamb; either signs of the promise or appointment made between God and man, as circumcision; or signs that testify unto the people that the wrath of God is peaced, and their sins forgiven, as all manner sacrifices: which all ceased as soon as Christ had offered up the sacrifice of his body and blood for us; and instead of them come the open preaching of Christ, and our signs which we call sacraments.[2]

The Christian is also bound by this covenant to live as a true child of God, who through his prayers keeps in touch with his heavenly Father. In *Mammon*, he outlines some of the difficulties that the Christian faces in his life. "Prayer is a mourning, a longing, and a desire of the spirit to God-ward, for that which she lacketh; . . . Faith ever prayeth."[3] In this way, man's spirit, through faith, longs and struggles for spiritual health so that it can truly honour and hallow God.

The spirit waiteth and watcheth on the will of God, and ever hath her own fragility and weakness before her eyes; and when she seeth temptation and peril draw nigh, she turneth to God, and to the testament that God hath made to all that believe and trust in Christ's blood; and desireth God for his mercy and truth, and for the love that he hath to Christ, that he will fulfil his promise.[4]

1. William Tyndale, *Sacraments, PS-1*, p. 350.
2. William Tyndale, *Prelates, PS-2*, p. 324.
3. William Tyndale, *Mammon, PS-1*, p. 93.
4. Ibid., p. 93.

Thus, God gives us his succour and strength so that we may keep the covenant faithfully.

Tyndale believed that this covenant is most important for us if we are to know that we are God's elect children, even if it appears that everyone is against us, as we have seen,

> And thereto, if it were possible that all the angels of heaven could be mine enemies, yet would I hold me by the testament that my merciful and true Father hath made me in the blood of my Saviour, and so come unto all that is promised me, and Christ hath purchased for me, and give not a straw for them all.[1]

The danger lies when we do not recognise the full meaning of God's covenant to us in the scriptures; when we do not believe the importance of the blood of Christ and when we try to do something ourselves towards our salvation. "When the covenant made in the blood of Christ, is blinded: then men pain themselves with holy works, trusting thereby to enter: but all in vain."[2] For God makes it clear that we have to receive everything for our salvation from Him and that we are powerless to do anything ourselves.

In a long paragraph in *The Sacraments of Baptism and of the Body and Blood of Christ,* Tyndale expresses the differences between the old covenant before Christ shed his blood, and the new covenant that started with Christ's sacrificial blood being shed when he was crucified.

> Moses offered half the blood to God, and sprinkled the people with the other half, to confirm the covenant and to bind both parties: neither was there any covenant made that was not confirmed with blood, as it is rehearsed in Hebrews ix.; and as we see in the books of Moses, whose custom of blood-shedding was not only to confirm those old covenants, but also to be a prophecy of the blood that should be shed to confirm this testament.

Tyndale then wrote of the people's fear of the thunder and fire when God made the covenant with them at Mount Sinai, and also that the people were not allowed to come near the mountain, even though the covenant

> was confirmed with the blood of calves: but this new and gentle testament, which calleth again, and promiseth mercy to all that will amend, as it is a better testament, so is it confirmed with a better blood, to make men see love, to love again, and to be a greater confirmation of the love promised.[3]

1. William Tyndale, *Answer, PS-3*, p. 89 (see fn. 5).
2. William Tyndale, *1534, New Testament*, mg. note, Lk. 13.
3. William Tyndale, *Sacraments, PS-1*, p. 364.

God's work to restore creation to its pristine state required the restoration of man to life and the destruction of Satan. To achieve this, the Persons of God the Trinity made a covenant between themselves. God the Son took the responsibility of destroying the power of Satan and, through his sacrificial blood, paying man's debt to the Trinity. This enabled the Father to be a Father to man, who had been re-created and empowered by the Holy Spirit to become a child of God.

3. The Fall to Man's Freedom From Slavery

In this chapter, we start with Adam's disobedience to God's command as he yielded to Satan's temptation, and we begin to see God working to bring about the restoration of man and the world to His rule. But first, Adam had to be punished for having sinned when he broke God's command. We trace the unfolding of God's plan for man's salvation and God's choice of Abraham and his children to bring about this salvation. The chapter ends when the chosen people, having been enslaved in Egypt (symbolising man's slavery to Satan), were set free through the sacrifice of the Paschal lamb.

Creation and the Fall of Man

The creation of man is mentioned by Tyndale only as a fact; his concern is more with the state of man after the Fall and God's dealing with man to restore man to fellowship with himself. God had told man that if he broke the one command that he had given to him, that is, to taste the fruit of the tree of knowledge of good and evil, he would die. But Adam and Eve broke that commandment and died spiritually. Sin entered the world and the world was cursed; and Satan became god of the world.

> As thou readest, therefore, think that every syllable pertaineth to thine own self, and suck out the pith of the scripture, and arm thyself against all assaults. First note with strong faith the power of God, in creating all of nought; and mark the grievous fall of Adam, and of us all in him, through the light regarding of the commandment of God.[1]

But, as we have seen, God planned to restore the world to its pristine glory, and this meant forgiving man for the sin that he had committed and creating him anew. By breaking God's commandment, Adam brought man into spiritual death, separating him from God. As a result, man became a slave to Satan, who, through man's sin, became the ruler of the world.

God told Satan that he was going to put enmity between Adam's seed and the Devil's seed. Many years later, God told Abraham that one of his

1. William Tyndale, *The Use of Scripture, PS-1*, p. 400.

seed would destroy Satan's power. When God told Abraham to sacrifice his son, Isaac, Isaac asked his father, "'Behold, the fire and the wood: but where is the lamb for a burnt offering?' And Abraham said, 'God will provide himself the lamb for a burnt offering.'" But, Isaac did not have to be sacrificed because a ram was caught in a nearby thicket, and this was sacrificed instead of Isaac (Gen. 22:1-19).

> Abraham through works was sure of his faith to be right, and that the true fear of God was in him, when he had offered his son: as the scripture saith, 'Now know I that thou fearest God;' that is to say, Now is it open and manifest that thou fearest God, inasmuch as thou has not spared thy only son for my sake.[1]

Tyndale links Christ to the seed that was promised to Abraham, when he wrote in his *Answer to Sir Thomas More*,

> Christ asked the apostles (Matt. xvi.) whom they took him for. And Peter answered for them all, saying, "I say that thou art Christ, the Son of the living God, that art come into this world." That is, We believe that thou art he that was promised unto Abraham, that should come, bless us, and deliver us. Howbeit, Peter yet wist not, by what means. But now it is opened throughout all the world, that, through his offering of his body and blood, that offering is a satisfaction for the sin of all that repent, and a purchasing of whatsoever they can ask, to keep them in favour; and that they sin no more."[2]

Tyndale wrote that every human being is a child of God through creation. This makes a problem for some academics as Tyndale seems, at times, to teach universalism.[3] However, a careful reading of Tyndale's writings shows that he was not a universalist, every man is created by God, but not every man is re-created through Christ's blood. Tyndale is clearest in *Pathway* where he wrote about the difference between man, as created, and the Christian, as man re-created. "And inasmuch as he is our Lord and God, and we his double possession, by creation and redemption."[4]

> God careth for his, and ministereth all things unto them, and moveth Turks, and Saracens, and all manner infidels to do them good: as thou seest in Abraham, Isaac, and Jacob, and how God went with Joseph into Egypt, and gat him favour in the prison, and in every place; which

1. William Tyndale, *Mammon, PS-1*, p. 60f.
2. William Tyndale, *Answer, PS-3*, p. 31.
3. J. Wayne Baker, *Heinrich Bullinger and the Covenant*, p. 209: For Tyndale 'the covenant idea was implicitly, if not always explicitly, universalist.' Quoted in my *The Theology of William Tyndale*, p. 78.
4. William Tyndale, *Pathway, PS-1*, p. 24.

favour Joseph received of the hand of God, and to God gave the thanks thus is God and Christ all in all; good and bad receive I of God. Them that are good I love, because they are in Christ; and the evil, to bring them to Christ. . . . Finally, inasmuch as God hath created all, and Christ bought all with his blood, therefore ought all to seek God and Christ in all, and else nothing.[1]

Again, Tyndale wrote, we must love our neighbours, "because God hath created them unto his likeness, and Christ hath redeemed them and bought them with his blood."[2]

Tyndale narrowed the scope a little when he wrote, "God hath created us and made us unto his own likeness; and our Saviour Christ hath bought us with his blood."[3] For even though everyone has been "created after his [God's] image," and are "the price of his [Christ's] blood", Tyndale limited its application to those who had faith in Christ's sacrificial blood on the Cross. "For faith in Christ's blood (which is God's promise) quieteth the conscience of all true believers."

Tyndale's emphasis that we are to help our neighbours because they are the price of Christ's blood covers every human being. This has an importance for us, because we do not know who is one of God's elect – for it is not for us to judge people, whether they are Turks or Saracens, or who has, and who has not, been elected by God for salvation.

In his 'Prologue' to the *1525 New Testament*, Tyndale wrote about the Fall of Adam and about Christ's blood setting us free from the result of the Fall:

The fall of Adam hath made us heirs of the vengeance and wrath of God, and heirs of eternal damnation. And hath brought us into captivity and bondage under the devil. And the devil is our lord, and our ruler, our head, our governor, our prince, yea, and our god. . . . It is not possible for a natural man to consent to the law, that it should be good, or that God should be righteous, which maketh the law. Man's wit, reason, and will, are so fast glued, yea, nailed and chained unto the will of the devil. Neither can any creature loose the bonds, save the blood of Christ. This is the captivity and bondage whence Christ delivered us, redeemed, and loosed us.[4]

Adam's disobedience had resulted in a barrier between God and man; and Adam gave to the Devil his power to rule and take care of the world. Therefore, God had to devise a plan to destroy Satan and end his dominion over the world and also to restore creation to its original glory and man to his life and fellowship with God.

1. William Tyndale, *Obedience, PS-1*, p. 298f.
2. William Tyndale, *Prologue Matthew, PS-1*, p. 470.
3. William Tyndale, *Answer, PS-3*, p. 57.
4. William Tyndale, *1525, New Testament*, pp. 9, 10.

God's creation culminated in the creation of man, but Tyndale is concerned more with the state of man after the Fall and with God's dealing with man; God's purpose was to destroy the Devil and break his hold over man. He was going to re-create man and restore creation to the pristine goodness that it had before the Fall. Tyndale describes the outworking of God's plan through Christ's blood thus:

> This is the captivity and bondage whence Christ delivered us, redeemed and loosed us. His blood, his death, [and his ministry on earth, and fulfilling of God's law] peaced the wrath of God, brought the favour of God to us again, obtained that God should . . . be our Father, and that a merciful Father; . . . and will give us his Spirit again (which was taken away in the fall of Adam) to rule, govern, and strength us, and to break the bonds of Satan wherein we were so strait bound.[1]

This leads us straight into God's salvation of man from the power of Satan and from the spiritual death that resulted from Adam's sin.

The beginning of Man's restoration

> In Gen. iii. God saith to the serpent, "I will put hatred between thee and the woman, between thy seed and her seed; that self seed shall tread thy head underfoot." Christ is this woman's seed: he it is that hath trodden underfoot the devil's head, that is to say, sin, death, hell, and all his power. For without this seed can no man avoid sin, death, hell, and everlasting damnation.[2]

The next step in God's plan was to choose Abraham and his seed, through which God would achieve his plan for man's salvation.

> For he promised Abraham, that in his Seed all the world should be blessed from the curse of sin; and hath abundantly renewed his everlasting mercy unto us in the new Testament, promising that our sins shall be forgiven us in Christ's blood, if we repent, and trust thereto.[3]

However, Abraham's children had a long and difficult journey before that seed should come into the world, and, of Abraham's descendants, Israel was chosen to inherit God's promise. It was a journey that led to Israel's children becoming a nation, and who became slaves to Pharaoh in Egypt; even as all mankind had, through Adam's disobedience, become slaves to the Devil.

---

1. Ibid., p. 10.
2. William Tyndale, *Pathway, PS-1*, p. 10: see also, *1525, New Testament*, p. 3.
3. William Tyndale, *Exposition, 1 John, PS-2*, p. 150.

Joseph saw the sun and moon and the eleven stars worshipping him. Nevertheless, ere that came to pass, God laid him where he could neither see sun nor moon, neither star in the sky, and that many years; and also undeserved; to nurture him, to humble, to meek, and to teach him God's ways.[1]

Eventually, Joseph's father, Israel, went down to Egypt with his family, and they prospered until a pharaoh, who did not recognise what Joseph had done for the people of Egypt, came to rule the Egyptians and enslaved them. The children of Israel became slaves in Egypt. The pharaoh oppressed them and made them produce bricks for his buildings. They had no freedom, and to prevent them from getting too powerful, the pharaoh decreed that every baby boy was to be drowned in the River Nile. "How wonderfully were the children of Israel locked in Egypt! In what tribulation, cumbrance, and adversity were they in![2] However, baby Moses was saved; he was brought up in the pharaoh's household, before he fled from Egypt and lived in the Sinai Peninsula. Eventually, Moses was sent by God to rescue the Israelites from their slavery. But that seemed to make the Israelites' position worse, and the burden placed on them became even greater. But then, God sent his plagues on the Egyptians, until finally the pharaoh told the Israelites to leave Egypt.

When God was about to send His last plague and slay the first-born of man and beast in Egypt, He provided a way for the first-born of the children of Israel to be saved. God told them to slay a kid or a lamb and to put its blood on the door-posts of their house. The annual Passover festival enabled the Israelites to remember their deliverance from slavery. It was at the end of the Passover meal that Jesus instituted the Lord's Supper. The Passover

> was also a very prophecy of the passion of Christ, describing the very manner and fashion of his death, and the effect and virtue thereof also. In whose stead is the sacrament of the body and blood of Christ come, as baptism in the room or stead of circumcision. To see how Christ was prophesied and described therein, consider and mark, how that the kid or lamb must be without spot or blemish; and so was Christ only of all mankind, in the sight of God and his law.[3]

Tyndale was more concerned with God's redemption of man from Satan's bondage than with the redemption of the Jews from their slavery under the pharaoh, as is made clear in *Mammon.*

---

1. William Tyndale, *Obedience, PS-1*, p. 136.

2. Ibid., p. 134.

3. William Tyndale, *Sacraments, PS-1*, p. 354.

In Christ's blood are we blessed from that bitter curse and damnable captivity under sin, wherein we were born and conceived. And Christ's Spirit is poured into us, to bring forth good works, and our works are the fruits of the Spirit; and the kingdom is the deserving of Christ's blood; and so is faith, and the Spirit, and good works also.[1]

When Jesus and his disciples were in the Upper Room to celebrate the Passover, Jesus taught his disciples its true meaning (Lk. xxii.):

For the night before his passion, when he had eaten Pesah with his disciples, he said, "I will no more eat of it henceforth, till it be fulfilled in the kingdom of God." As who should say, 'This memorial which we yearly have hitherto observed, was once fulfilled in the kingdom of this world, when your fathers were delivered out of bondage and servitude of the Egyptians. But it hath yet another signification, hitherto unknown to you, which must be fulfilled spiritually in the kingdom of God by my passion that is at hand, and blood that now shall shortly be shed; by the which ye shall be delivered out of the power of Satan, sin, and hell, and made heirs of the kingdom of heaven. Neither was it the lambs blood that delivered you then: (for what regard hath God in the blood of sheep and calves?) but the blood of Christ (whom that lamb figured, and described his innocence, pureness, and obedience to his Father, and compassion to mankind-ward, whose feeble nature he had put on with all the infirmities of the same, save sin) did then deliver you, to bring you to the faith of this deliverance, and make you through faith partakers thereof.[2]

Tyndale then shows that the date of the slaying of the Passover lamb and of putting its blood on the door-posts (celebrated by the Jews every year) signified the Holy Spirit's sprinkling Christ's blood on the door-posts of our conscience, which happened at the Passover meal with the institution of the Lord's Supper.

The blood stricken on the posts saved them, that they were not plagued with the Egyptians, and delivered them out of the captivity of Pharao. And the blood of Christ, striken on the posts of our consciences with a sure faith, delivereth us from the captivity of Pharao the devil, and smiting of his angels.[3]

Tyndale tells us the importance of the Old Testament scriptures, for we need to learn from the history of the Israelites, so that we (Christians) do not make the same kind of mistakes in our worship of God.

---

1. William Tyndale, *Mammon, PS-1*, p. 83.
2. William Tyndale, *Sacraments, PS-1*, p. 355.
3. Ibid., p. 354.

These are ensamples written for our learning (as Paul saith), to teach us to trust in God in the strong fire of tribulation and purgatory of our flesh; and that they which submit themselves to follow God, should note and mark such things: for their learning and comfort is the fruit of the scripture, and cause why it was written. And with such a purpose to read it, is the way to everlasting life, and to those joyful blessings that are promised unto all nations in the Seed of Abraham: which Seed is Jesus Christ our Lord, to whom be honour and praise for ever, and unto God our Father through him.[1]

After the Israelites had been freed from Pharaoh's bondage, they had to journey through the wilderness to reach the Promised Land:

The land also that was promised them was far off, and full of great cities, walled with high walls up to the sky, and inhabited with great giants; yet God's truth brought them out of Egypt, and planted them in the land of the giants. This was also written for our learning: for there is no power against God's, neither any wisdom against God's wisdom: he is stronger and wiser than all his enemies. What holp it Pharaoh, to drown the men children? So little (I fear not) shall it at the last help the pope and his bishops, to burn our men children; which manfully confess that Jesus Christ is the Lord, and that there is no other name given unto men to be saved by, as Peter testifieth, Acts, in the fourth chapter.[2]

Because we have been freed from our slavery to Satan's power and of our desire and willingness to sin by the Holy Spirit's sprinkling us with the blood of Christ, we are set free to love and serve God.

And therefore Paul saith, "If the Spirit of him that raised up Jesus from death be in you, then will he that raised up Jesus from death quicken your mortal bodies by the reason of the Spirit that dwelleth in you." So that it is not possible for him that knoweth the truth, and consenteth thereto, to continue in sin. And then, finally, if we have the light in our hearts, and walk therein, then we have fellowship with God, and are his sons and heirs, and are purged from all sin through Christ's blood.[3]

Tyndale tells us that God's hand was behind the history of the Israelites, so that they could learn the spiritual reality behind the events that affected their everyday life. But the events that affected the Children of Israel,

---

1. William Tyndale, *Prologue Genesis, PS-1*, p. 402f.
2. William Tyndale, *Obedience, PS-1*, p. 134.
3. William Tyndale, *Exposition 1 John, PS-2*, p. 149.

especially up to their entry into the Promised Land, were to help Christians in their spiritual journey. The importance of the Israelites' journey for the Christian is clear in Paul's First Epistle to the Corinthians (10:1-13), where he draws our attention to some events on their journey: "Now these things were our examples" (v. 6).

4. Man's Salvation

We have seen how, through Adam's disobedience to God's commandment, man became enslaved to Satan and was powerless to do anything that was pleasing to God. But God, through his love and mercy, planned man's liberation to set him free through the shedding of the blood of God's Son. The first period of man's salvation was before the Son of God became man, and so God ordained animals to be sacrificed, and their sacrificial blood would stand for the blood of Christ, which, one day, would be shed for the forgiveness of sin. After Christ's blood was shed on the Cross, the sacrificing of animals was no longer necessary and they ceased. No longer were the Israelites alone God's chosen people, but it became possible for every human being, through a new birth, to be a child of God the Father. Christ's death destroyed Satan's power and restored creation, and Christ's blood benefited the Gentiles. And so, God made it possible for every man, through the blood of Christ, to be born again as a child of God.

In the 'Prologue' to his 1525 translation of the New Testament, Tyndale leads us from God's promise after the Fall to God's promise to Abraham after he had shown his obedience to God that he was prepared to offer his only son as a sacrifice to God.

> In the third chapter of Genesis, God saith to the serpent: "I will put hatred between thee and the woman, between thy seed and her seed, that self seed shall tread thy head under foot." Christ is this woman's seed, he it is that hath trodden under foot the devil's head; that is to say, sin, death, hell and all his power, For without this seed can no man avoid sin, death, hell, and everlasting damnation. Again, Gen. xxii. God promised Abraham saying: "In thy seed shall all generations of the earth be blessed." Christ is that seed of Abraham saith saint Paul in the third to the Galatians. He hath blessed all the world through the gospel. For where Christ is not, there remaineth the curse that fell on Adam as soon as he had sinned. So that they are in bondage under the domination of sin, death, and hell.[1]

---

1. William Tyndale, *1525, New Testament*, p. 3.

We have seen that those who benefit from Christ's death, the seed of Abraham, are those who have been chosen by God, those who are the elect to become the children of God (Chapter 2). In this chapter, we will see how God enables the elect to be his children and bring them from being 'dead in trespasses and sins' to life as part of God's family.

From Death to Life

When God created man, he gave man "dominion" over all living things "and over all the earth," and God gave man "every green herb for meat". However, there was one tree that Adam must not eat, "of the tree of the knowledge of good and evil, thou shalt not eat of it: for in the day that thou eatest thereof thou shalt surely die." (Gen. 2:17). However, Adam ate of the tree and, as a result, Adam and Eve died spiritually. Tyndale quotes from Paul's Epistle to the Ephesians (Chapter 2): "Ye were dead in trespasses and sin, in which ye walked according to the course of the world, and after the governor that ruleth in the air, . . ." Tyndale continues,

> The text is plain: we were stone dead, and without life or power to do or consent to good. The whole nature of us was captive under the devil, and led at his will. And we were as wicked as the devil now is; . . . and we consented unto sin with soul and body, and hated the law of God.[1]

We have, therefore, to be born again, or be created anew, by God so that we have passed from death to life (Jn 3:14). "We be all equally created and formed of one God our Father, and indifferently bought and redeemed with one blood of our Saviour Jesus Christ."[2]

There was a debt that had to be paid to the Trinity because of Adam's sin, and the scripture makes it clear that man is incapable of paying that debt. Jesus Christ, God's Son, alone was able to pay that debt and to be the Saviour of the world.

> And John, in the first chapter, "Behold the Lamb of God which taketh away the sin of the world:" which sin was the bush which stopped the entering in, and kept us out; and the sword wherewith was kept the entering unto the tree of life from Adam and all his offspring. And in the second of the first of Peter, "which bare our sins in his body," and, "by whose stripes we are made whole." "By whom we have redemption through his blood, even the forgiveness of our sins" (Colos. i. and Ephes. i.)[3]

1. William Tyndale, *Exposition 1 John, PS-2*, p. 199.
2. William Tyndale, *Prologue, Jonas, PS-1*, p. 464.
3. William Tyndale, *'Tracy, PS-3*, p. 274.

In his *Exposition of the First Epistle of St. John*, Tyndale warns his readers of how the pope's Church erroneously believes that man himself can make satisfaction for sin: "Whereas the scripture saith, Christ is our righteousness, our justifying, our redemption, our atonement, that hath appeased God, and cleanseth us from our sins, and all in his blood, so that his blood is the satisfaction only."[1]

God chose Abraham and promised that, through Abraham's seed, God would restore man to the state he had before Adam disobeyed God's commandment. God's covenant was to destroy Satan's power and restore creation to its pristine state. To do this, God had to restore life to those who were dead in trespasses and sin. In the beginning, God had "created us of nought, and heaven and earth for our sakes; and afterwards when we had marred ourself through sin, he forgave us, and created us again, in the blood of his beloved Son."[2] Tyndale repeated this in his *Answer*: "God hath created us and made us unto his own likeness; and our Saviour Christ hath bought us with his blood."[3] On several occasions, Tyndale enlarged on this, and in his *1526 New Testament* "Epistle to the Reader", he wrote,

I exhort thee, that thou come with a pure mind, and, as the scripture saith, with a single eye, unto the words of health and of eternal life; by the which, if we repent and believe them, we are born anew, created afresh, and enjoy the fruits of the blood of Christ: which blood crieth not for vengeance, as the blood of Abel, but hath purchased life, love, favour, grace, blessing, and whatsoever is promised in the scriptures to them that believe and obey God.[4]

A New Birth (Creation)

As we have seen (Chapter 3), Adam's Fall had left us slaves of the Devil, and we are unable to do anything not dictated to us by Satan. This means that if man is going to be set free, he must, as Jesus told Nicodemus, he must "be born anew" (Jn 3:5) "The Evangelion showeth unto him the promises of God in Christ, and how that Christ has purchased pardon for him, has satisfied the law for him, and peaced the wrath of God." Otherwise, he remains Satan's slave.[5] For

Christ, which is contrary to the devil, came to destroy the works of the devil in us, and to give us a new birth, a new nature, and to sow new

1. William Tyndale, *Exposition 1 John, PS-2*, p. 157.
2. William Tyndale, *Pathway, PS-1*, p. 24.
3. William Tyndale, *Answer, PS-3*, p. 57.
4. William Tyndale, *1526, New Testament, PS-1*, p. 389.
5. William Tyndale, *Prologue, 1525 New Testament*, p. 9.

seed in us, that we should, by the reason of that birth, sin no more. For the seed of that birth, that is to wete the Spirit of God and the lively seed of his word sown in our hearts, keepeth our hearts, that we cannot consent to sin.[1]

The only way man can be set free from his slavery is through Christ's blood.

It is not possible for a natural man to consent to the law, that it should be good, or that God should be righteous, which maketh the law. Man's wit, reason, and will, are so fast glued, yea, nailed and chained unto the will of the devil. Neither can any creature loose the bonds, save the blood of Christ. This is the captivity and bondage whence Christ delivered us, redeemed and loosed us. His blood, his death, his patience, . . . peaced the wrath of God, brought the favour of God to us again, obtained that God should love us first, and be our Father, and that a merciful Father.[2]

The New Life

Although we will be considering some key theological words, we must remember that they cannot be separated one from another. Some of the overlaps will be seen in the quotations from Tyndale's writings, and there will be times when one aspect of our life as a child of God seems more important than other aspects. But, as with our physical life, we cannot isolate one action from many other actions that our body performs at the same time.

Once a man has been born anew through the Holy Spirit's sprinkling of Christ's blood[3] on the elect, he has a new life as a child of God. This new life depends on our faith in the work Christ did for our salvation, and Christ's sacrificial blood is still needed to cleanse and keep clean every aspect of man's life. For

Christ came only therefore in the flesh, that he should justify us, or purchase us pardon of our sins, bring us in the favour of God again, and make us heirs of eternal life with his works only, and with his blood-shedding, without and before all our works.[4]

Therefore, the Christian must

believe as the gospel, glad tidings and promises of God say unto thee; that for Christ's blood's sake only, through faith, God is at one with

---

1. William Tyndale, *Exposition 1 John, PS-2*, p. 190.
2. William Tyndale, *Prologue, 1525 New Testament*, p. 10.
3. Sprinkling the sacrificial blood in the Old Testament was the normal way to make the sacrifice effective. See also, Heb. 9:11-28.
4. William Tyndale, *Prologue upon the three Epistles of John, PS-1*, p. 530.

thee, and thou received to mercy, and art become the son of God, and heir annexed with Christ of all the goodness of God; the earnest whereof is the Spirit of God poured into our hearts.[1]

Tyndale was following the link between the sacrifices in the Old Testament and Christ's sacrifice:

As it is rehearsed in Hebrews ix.; and as we see in the books of Moses, whose custom of blood-shedding was not only to confirm those old covenants, but also to be a prophecy of the blood that should be shed to confirm this testament.[2]

Repentance and faith are basic to salvation, and without them man remains dead in bondage to the Devil; they are the first two steps we can make after we are born anew. Repentance and faith must continue throughout the whole of our Christian life so that, "by the means of the blood of Jesus, we may be bold to enter into the holy place, by the new and living way, which he hath prepared for us, through the veil, that is to say by his flesh." (Heb. 10:19, 20).

For the scripture testifieth that Christ hath taken away the sin of the world in his flesh; and that at the same hour that he yielded up his spirit into the hands of his Father, he had full purged, and made full satisfaction for all the sins of the world: so that all the sin of the world, both before his passion and after, must be put away through repentance toward the law, and faith and trust in his blood, without respect of any other satisfaction, sacrifice, or work.[3]

Repentance and faith are signs of life during the Christian's time on earth, for some remnants of sin still remain in him, which need to be cleansed with the blood of Christ.

For if I once sin, the law rebuketh my conscience, and setteth variance between God and me: and I shall never be at peace with God again, until I have heard the voice of his mouth, how that my sin is forgiven me for Christ's blood's sake.[4]

The Christian finds that peace with God as he "goeth through repentance toward the law unto the faith that is in Christ's blood."[5] For although repentance marks the beginning of our life as a child of God, it has to be

1. William Tyndale, *Mammon, PS-1*, p. 71.
2. William Tyndale, *Sacraments, PS-1*, p. 364 (see also Chapter 1, p.).
3. William Tyndale, *Exposition 1 John, PS-2*, p. 196.
4. Ibid., p. 196.
5. William Tyndale, *Answer, PS-3*, p. 193.

part of our continuing Christian life whilst we remain on earth, because "when we have sinned, we go with a repenting heart unto Christ's blood, and there wash it off through faith."[1]

Repentance

"When a true preacher preacheth, the Spirit entereth the hearts of the elect, and maketh them feel the righteousness of the law of God, and by the law the poison of their corrupt nature; and thence leadeth them, through repentance, unto the mercy that is in Christ's blood."[2] For it is "the faith of a repenting soul in Christ's blood doth justify only."[3]

Tyndale commenced his "Epistle to the Reader" in his first printed New Testament, published in 1526, by showing the importance of repentance, and of believing God's word given us in the New Testament.[4] For all the teaching and ceremonies of the papal Church are 'dumb' and cannot bring us holiness or salvation. What is needed is "the holiness of God's word; which only speaketh unto the heart, and sheweth the soul his filthiness and uncleanness of sin, and leadeth her by the way of repentance unto the fountain of Christ's blood, to wash it away through faith."[5] For "the scripture saith, that we be justified at the repentance of the heart, through Christ's blood."[6]

Several times in his *Answer to Sir Thomas More's Dialogue*, Tyndale wrote about the need for a child of God to have a 'repenting heart': "To believe in Christ's blood with a repenting heart is to make righteous, and the only making of peace and satisfaction to God-ward."[7]

Faith

Faith has supreme importance in the Christian life, for every other aspect of our salvation depends on faith. Tyndale criticised the spiritualty who "have clean excluded the faith in the satisfaction of Christ's blood; which only bringeth life, and the spirit of life, and righteousness, and without the which it is impossible to please God."[8] Here, Tyndale was referring to Hebrews

---

1. Ibid., p. 204.
2. William Tyndale, *Exposition 1 John, PS-2*, p. 183f.
3. William Tyndale, *Answer, PS-3*, p. 172.
4. See p. 41 fn. 4. 'Give diligence, reader, I exhort thee, that thou come with a pure mind, and, as the scripture saith, with a single eye, unto the words of health and of eternal life; by the which, if we repent and believe them, we are born anew, created afresh, and enjoy the fruits of the blood of Christ.' *Tyndale's Epistle to the Reader, 1526, PS-1*, p. 389.
5. William Tyndale, *Prologue to Jonas, PS-1*, p. 462.
6. William Tyndale, *Answer, PS-3*, p. 111.
7. Ibid., p. 206; see also, pp. 111, 149, 196, 197; *Exposition 1 John, PS-2*, p. 137.
8. William Tyndale, *Exposition 1 John, PS-2*, p. 162.

11:6: Enoch "had pleased God: but without faith it is unpossible to please him. For he that cometh to God, must believe that God is, and that he is a rewarder of them that seek him."

Baptism is the God-given sign of our becoming a child of God[1] and represents our commitment to God, for

> to believe in Christ's blood for the remission of sin, and purchasing of all the good promises that help to the life to come; and to love the law; and to long for the life to come, is the inward baptism of the soul, the baptism that only availeth in the sight of God.[2]

Tyndale expands on the ways in which baptism affects our Christian life and the knowledge that we need for our life as God's children.

In the parable of the Marriage Feast, there was a man who had not a "wedding-garment" (Mt. 22:11), which would have been given to each of the guests, and Tyndale, following the paragraph on the "inward baptism of the soul," wrote,

> And though faith in Christ's blood make the marriage between our soul and Christ, and is properly the marriage garment; . . . yet might the profession of faith in Christ's blood, and of the love to the law, and longing for the life to come, be called all these things.[3]

Faith is not something that is naturally found in man, for until he is born again, he is dead and cannot respond to the Gospel being preached. Faith is given to us by God's Holy Spirit, as Tyndale wrote,

> But right faith is a thing wrought by the Holy Ghost in us, which changeth us, turneth us into a new nature, and begetteth us anew in God, and maketh us the sons of God, as thou readest in the first of John; and killeth the old Adam, and maketh us altogether new in the heart, mind, will, lust, and in all our affections and powers of the soul; the Holy Ghost ever accompanying her, and ruling the heart.[4]

The fact that faith comes from God through Christ's blood also seems to lie behind Tyndale's words in his *Prologue to the 1525 New Testament*, although after writing, "Now Christ standeth us in double stead, and serveth us two manner wise. First he is our redeemer, his blood, his death, all that he ever did is ours. And Christ himself will all that he is or can do, is ours. His blood is shedding does me as good service as if I had done it myself . . . Secondarily, after we be overcome with love and kindness, and now seek to

1. See Chapter 5, p. 68 ff.
2. William Tyndale, *Exposition Matthew, PS-2*, p. 13.
3. Ibid.
4. William Tyndale, *Prologue Romans, PS-1*, p. 493.

do the will of God. . . . Then have we Christ an ensample to counterfeit."[1] Tyndale expresses this idea in *Obedience*: "If he believe in Christ, then is he a member of Christ, Christ's brother, Christ's flesh, Christ's blood, Christ's spouse, coheir with Christ, and hath his Spirit in earnest, and is also spiritual."[2] The second part is our response in following Christ's example; when he wrote, "Whatsoever therefore faith hath received of God through Christ's blood and deserving, that same must love shed out every whit, and bestow it on our neighbours unto their profit."[3]

We must hold fast to our faith, for that is necessary for our justification and for our salvation; therefore, Tyndale wrote, "tie to thy ship this anchor of faith in Christ's blood with the cable of love, to cast it out against all tempests; and so set up thy sail, and get thee to the main sea of God's word."[4]

It is through Christ's blood that the work of the Holy Spirit in us became a possibility, as we feel drawn inwardly to live a Christian life, Tyndale wrote, that if

> we be merciful to the poor, for conscience to God, and of compassion and hearty love, which compassion and love spring of the love we have to God in Christ, for the pure mercy and love that he hath shewed on us: then have we a sure token that we are beloved of God, and washed in Christ's blood, and elect, by Christ's deserving, unto eternal life.[5]

Then, through the Holy Spirit's indwelling, we can do the good works that God requires of us. "Even so now since I am coupled to God by Christ's blood, do I well, not for heaven's sake: but because I am heir of heaven by grace and Christ's purchasing, and have the Spirit of God, I do good freely, for so is my nature.[6]

Justification

Although justification by faith was important to Tyndale, we must not think that every Reformer understood 'justification by faith' in the same way. Tyndale wrote, "In the gospel when we believe the promises, we receive the Spirit of life, and are justified in the blood of Christ from all things whereof the law condemned us."[7] Alister McGrath wrote that Tyndale's understanding of justification by faith differed from Luther's understanding:

1. William Tyndale, *1525, New Testament*, p. 11.
2. William Tyndale, *Obedience, PS-1*, p. 240.
3. William Tyndale, *1525, New Testament*, p. 11.
4. William Tyndale, *Exposition Matthew, PS-2*, p. 15.
5. William Tyndale, *Mammon, PS-1*, p. 107.
6. William Tyndale, *1525, New Testament*, p. 14.
7. Ibid., p. 4.

William Tyndale, although making extensive use of Luther in his early polemical works, tends to interpret justification as 'making righteous'. Tyndale's emphasis upon the renewing and transforming work of the Holy Spirit within man is quite distinct from Luther's emphasis upon faith.[1]

Tyndale explained quite simply what he understood by justification by faith in his "Prologue" to his *Exposition of Matthew v. vi, vii.*

> The faith of the true believers is, that God justifieth or forgiveth; and Christ deserveth it; and the faith or trust in Christ's blood receiveth it, and certifieth the conscience thereof, and saveth and delivereth her from fear of death and damnation. And this is that we mean, when we say faith justifieth: that faith (I mean in Christ, and not in our own works) certifieth the conscience that our sins are forgiven us for Christ's blood's sake.[2]

Tyndale also wrote about justification by faith in his *Answer to Sir Thomas More*: "Hereof ye see what faith it is that justifieth us. The faith in Christ's blood, of a repenting heart toward the law, doth justify us only; and not all manner faiths."[3] Earlier, in his *Answer*, Tyndale wrote of its importance if we are to understand the scriptures: "I say, it is impossible to understand either Peter or Paul, or aught at all in the scripture, for him that denieth the justifying of faith in Christ's blood."[4]

In his *Prologue to the Book of Exodus*, Tyndale wrote that it was erroneous to think that Church ceremonies were able to justify us. Even the God-given ceremonies of the Old Testament "were not given to justify the heart, but to signify the justifying and forgiveness that is in Christ's blood."[5] He then quotes Hebrews 10:4, Galatians 3:21 and also draws our attention to 2 Corinthians 3.

Forgiveness

Faith is important for forgiveness, and in *Mammon*, Tyndale stresses the importance of God's promises:

> If thou wilt therefore be at peace with God, and love him, thou must turn to the promises of God, and to the gospel which is called of Paul, in the place before rehearsed to the Corinthians, the ministration of righteousness, and of the Spirit. For faith bringeth pardon and

---

1. Alister McGrath, *Iustitia Dei, vol 2*, p. 99.
2. William Tyndale, *Exposition Matthew, PS-2*, p. 11.
3. William Tyndale, *Answer, PS-3*, p. 196.
4. Ibid., p. 169.
5. William Tyndale, *Prologue Exodus, PS-1*, p. 416.

forgiveness freely purchased by Christ's blood, and bringeth also the Spirit; the Spirit looseth the bonds of the devil, and setteth us at liberty.[1]

This is also a continuation of God's promises in the Old Testament, for as we have seen in Chapter 3, God's promise to Abraham has been renewed to us in the New Testament, "promising that our sins shall be forgiven us in Christ's blood, if we repent, and trust thereto."[2] Tyndale turned to the sacrifices in the Old Testament, to the priesthood and to the sacrifices they offered to God:

> For Christ is Aaron and Aaron's sons, and all that offer the sacrifice to purge sin. And Christ is all manner offering that is offered; . . . for as they purged the people from their worldly uncleannesses through blood of the sacrifices, even so doth Christ purge us from the uncleannesses of everlasting death with his own blood; and as their worldly sin could no otherwise be purged, than by blood of sacrifices, even so can our sins be no otherwise forgiven than through the blood of Christ. All the deeds in the world, save the blood of Christ, can purchase no forgiveness of sins; . . . but and if we have sinned, it must be freely forgiven through the blood of Christ, or remain for ever.[3]

Tyndale, in *Answer*, warned us of the danger that faced us:

> And the stories of the old Testament are also by Paul, 1 Cor. x., our ensamples. And there, though God at a time called with miracles a great multitude, yet the very chosen that received the faith in their hearts, to put their trust in God alone, and which endureth on temptations, were but few.[4]

This leads on to Tyndale's teaching about the Church: the pope's Church, although being the largest, had drifted away from the truth and considered that man only had to do his best and God would forgive his shortcomings. However, the true Church is "the little flock" (Lk. 12:32), and they were forgiven through faith in Christ's blood.

> The preacher comforteth them, and sheweth them the testament of Christ's blood; how that for his sake all that is done is forgiven, and all their weakness shall be taken a worth, until they be stronger, only if they repent, and will submit themselves to be scholars, and learn to

---

1. William Tyndale, *Mammon, PS-1*, p. 48.
2. William Tyndale, *Exposition 1 John, PS-2*, p. 150.
3. William Tyndale, *Prologue Leviticus, PS-1*, p. 427.
4. William Tyndale, *Answer, PS-3*, p. 104.

keep the law. And little flock receiveth this testament in his heart, and in it walketh and serveth God in the spirit. And from henceforth all is Christ with him; and Christ is his, and he is Christ's.[1]

But there is a God-given condition for our forgiveness,[2] which Tyndale tells us in *Mammon*:

"If ye forgive other men their trespasses, your heavenly Father shall forgive you yours." Matt. in the vi. chap. If I forgive, God shall forgive me; not for my deeds sake, but for his promises' sake, for his mercy and truth, and for the blood of his Son, Christ our Lord.[3]

For we are to love our neighbour as we love ourself, as God has commanded us.

Bought with Christ's Blood

Tyndale frequently wrote about the cost of our salvation, for he could not think that man should accept salvation simply as a free gift from God; although it was given free to us, we must never forget the price that God paid for his gift:

Whatsoever is our own is sin. Whatsoever is above that is Christ's gift, purchase, doing, and working. He bought it of his Father dearly with his blood; yea, with his most bitter death and gave his life for it. Whatsoever good thing is in us, is given us freely without our deserving or merits, for Christ's blood's sake. That we desire to follow the will of God, it is the gift of Christ's blood. That we now hate the devil's will (whereunto we were so fast locked, and could not but love it) is also the gift of Christ's blood; unto whom belongeth the praise and honour of our good deeds and not unto us.[4]

In our Christian life, there are many things that demonstrate our Christian faith and are signs that our faith is real,

even so are all other good works outward signs and outward fruits of faith and of the Spirit; which justify not a man, but shew that a man is justified already before God, inwardly in the heart, through faith, and through the Spirit purchased by Christ's blood.[5]

---

1. Ibid., p. 108f.
2. Matthew 6:14, 15: "For if ye forgive men their trespasses, your heavenly Father will also forgive you. But if ye forgive not men their trespasses, neither will your Father forgive your trespasses."
3. William Tyndale, *Mammon, PS-1*, p. 76.
4. William Tyndale, *1525, New Testament*, p. 14.
5. William Tyndale, *Epistle to Romans, PS-1*, p. 497.

There are many other places where Tyndale speaks of 'being bought with Christ's blood', but they need to be considered in other contexts, especially in our Christian life and witness (we will consider them in the next chapter). "Finally, inasmuch as God hath created all, and Christ bought all with his blood, therefore ought all to seek God and Christ in all, and else nothing."[1]

Righteousness

We have already seen, in Tyndale's *1525 New Testament*, that we are "justified in the blood of Christ"[2] Now we begin to see how that justification works in our Christian life. It is in his earliest writing that we see the effect of Christ's blood for our salvation. Tyndale's marginal note on Matthew 21:32, in his *1525 New Testament*, speaks of 'righteousness': "John taught the very way unto righteousness; for he interpreted the law right; and damned man and all his deeds and righteousness: and drove men unto Christ to seek true righteousness through mercy obtained in his blood."[3]

According to Matthew 5, a Christian

> is an hungred and athirst after righteousness; for righteousness (I mean) which springeth out of Christ's blood, for strength to do the will of God; and turneth himself to the promises of God, and desireth him for his great mercy and truth, and for the blood of his Son Christ, to fulfil his promises, and to give him strength.[4]

Later in *Mammon*, Tyndale returns to that verse from Matthew 5: "God, for his truth's sake, must put the righteousness of Christ in him, and wash his unrighteousness away in the blood of Christ." Tyndale then spends time writing about the changes that take place in the heart and life of man when his being changes from a sinner to a child of God. he then continues, "His heart sinneth not, but mourneth, repenteth, and consenteth unto the law and will of God, and justifieth God; that is, beareth record that God which made the law is righteous and just. And such an heart, trusting in Christ's blood, is accepted for full righteous."[5]

Mercy and Favour

God has shown his mercy to those he has elected to be saved from Satan's power, and the child of God looks back to his liberation from slavery to the Devil, so that he does not despair. It is right at the very beginning of our life

---

1. William Tyndale, *Obedience, PS-1*, p. 299.
2. William Tyndale, *1525, New Testament*, p. 4.
3. Ibid., p. 61.
4. William Tyndale, *Mammon, PS-1*, p. 75.
5. Ibid., p. 94.

as a child of God that we experience God's mercy towards us. It is when man has realised that he is a sinner and as a result feels guilty and deserves to be totally rejected by God. For, wrote Tyndale,

> If a man had once felt within in his conscience the fierce wrath of God toward sinners, and the terrible and most cruel damnation that the law threateneth; and then beheld with the eyes of a strong faith the mercy, favour and grace, the taking away of the damnation of the law, and restoring again of life, freely offered us in Christ's blood, he should perceive love, and so much the more, that it was shewed us when we were sinners and enemies to God.[1]

Once the sinner has taken hold of God's promise, and, by repentance and faith, claims God's promise, God does not wait for him to prove that his repentance and faith are true, but immediately accepts him, for, "The scripture saith, that as soon as a man repenteth of evil, and believeth in Christ's blood, he obtaineth mercy immediately."[2] William Tracy, at the beginning of his Will, wrote,

> I commit me unto God, and to his mercy, trusting without any doubt or mistrust, that by his grace and merits of Jesus Christ, and by the virtue of his passion, and of his resurrection, I have and shall have remission of my sins, and resurrection of body and soul, according as it is written, (Job xiv.) "I believe that my Redeemer liveth, and that in the last day I shall rise out of the earth, and in my flesh shall see my Saviour." This my hope is laid up in my bosom.[3]

Tracy denied that his salvation depended on his good works, but that it was his duty to do those works in order to please God. Commenting on Tracy's will, Tyndale wrote, "If it be thy duty, how can it then be the deserving of the mercy and grace that went before? Now, that mercy was the benefit of God thy Father through the deserving of the Lord Christ, which hath bought thee with the price of his blood."[4]

Tyndale reminds us of the importance of remembering what God has done for us, and that we have to constantly remember what we owe to God for our salvation:

> I must also have the promises before my eyes, that I despair not, in which promises I see the mercy, favour, and good will of God upon me in the blood of his Son Christ; which has made satisfaction for my imperfections, and fulfilled for me that which I could not do.[5]

1. William Tyndale, *Exposition 1 John, PS-2*, p. 199.
2. William Tyndale, *Answer, PS-3*, p. 172.
3. William Tracy, *Exposition of Tracy's Testament, The Testament Itself, PS-3*, p. 272.
4. William Tyndale, *Exposition of Tracy's Testament, PS-3*, p. 277.
5. William Tyndale, *1525, New Testament*, p. 5.

Grace

Grace has an importance for the Christian's salvation. It tells us that there is nothing in fallen man that could cause God to forgive him of his sins, nor is there anything man can do that could open the way for God to be merciful to him. It is only through God's grace that we have been chosen to be His people.

Tyndale understands that no one deserves to be saved from his condemnation by God for his sin and for being a willing slave to Satan. Whilst the pope holds out to man the threat of purgatory, Tyndale wrote that God the Father has graciously reached out to man with His total forgiveness. "I say we that believe have no judge of him, but a Father, neither shall we come into judgement, as Christ hath promised us, but are received under grace, mercy and forgiveness." Therefore, there cannot be a purgatory "if I offer for me the blood of Christ."[1]

Neither can our salvation be earned through our good works or through the prayers of others, because we are doing those things that God demands of us. For we may not "ascribe to their merits that which is given us in the name of our master Christ, as the deservings of his blood. Christ is my Lord, and has deserved and also obtained power, to give me all that can be desired for me; and all that other desire for me, is desired in Christ's name, and given at the merits of his blood "[2]

Love

"We love, because he first loved us" (1 Jn 4:19). For man's salvation depends on his responding the God's love. Commenting on that verse, Tyndale wrote,

> We deserve not the love of God first; but he deserveth our love, and loveth us first, to win us, and to make us his friends of his enemies; and as soon as we believe his love we love again. And so faith is mother of all love: and as great as my faith is, so great is love, though faith cannot be perfectly seen, but through the works of love and in the fire of temptation.[3]

Tyndale tells us to "take an ensample in the great commandment, 'Love God with all thine heart,' the spiritual searcheth the cause, and looketh in the benefits of God, and so conceiveth love in heart." For love is a sign of his salvation. This love leads him on in his Christian life, for "he is commanded to obey the powers and rulers of the world, he looketh on the benefits which God sheweth the world through them, and therefore doth

1. William Tyndale, *Answer, PS-3*, p. 143.

2. William Tyndale, *Exposition Tracy's Will, PS-3*, p. 277f.

3. William Tyndale, *Exposition 1 John, PS-2*, p. 204.

it gladly." He is commanded also "to love his neighbour as himself," and because "his neighbour is created of God, and bought with Christ's blood," he loves him with his heart.[1]

Tyndale finds it impossible to separate those two commandments that summarise the law: to love God with heart, soul, mind and strength and to love our neighbour as ourselves. "If we felt the love of God in Christ's blood, we could not but love again, not only God and Christ, but also all that are bought with Christ's blood."[2]

Tyndale taught that a Christian's salvation also meant that he loved God's law. "And I feel that every soul that loveth the law, and hateth his flesh, and believeth in Christ's blood, hath his sins which he committed, and pain which he deserved, in hating the law and consenting unto his flesh, forgiven him by that faith."[3] It is through his love for the law that a Christian does good works. "The scripture saith, that as soon as a man repenteth of evil, and believeth in Christ's blood, he obtaineth mercy immediately, because he should love God, and of that love do good works."[4]

Child of God

God the Father (as we saw in Chapter 2) elected those who were to be his children, and "we are the sons of God; and that God hath chosen us, and washed us in Christ's blood; and hath put his Spirit in us."[5] The Christian realises the truth that this birth as God's child is, as his natural birth, something that is outside his power or control.

> Thou mayest not imagine that our deeds deserve the joy and glory that shall be given unto us; for then, Paul saith, Rom. xi. "Favour were not favour." I cannot receive it of favour and of the bounties of God, freely, and by deserving of deeds also. But believe as the gospel, glad tidings and promises of God say unto thee; that for Christ's blood's sake only, through faith, God is at one with thee and thou received to mercy, and art become the son of God, and heir annexed with Christ of all the goodness of God; the earnest whereof is the Spirit of God poured into our hearts. . . . Because I know God and testify the truth; then am I sure that God hath chosen me in Christ, and for Christ's sake, and hath put in me his Spirit, as an earnest of his promises, whose working I feel in my heart, the deeds bearing witness unto the same. Now is it Christ's blood only that deserveth all the promises of God.[6]

1. William Tyndale, *Answer, PS-3*, p. 6.
2. William Tyndale, *Exposition 1 John, PS-2*, p. 200.
3. William Tyndale, *Answer, PS-3*, p. 142.
4. Ibid., p. 172f.
5. William Tyndale, *Mammon, PS-1*, p. 72.
6. Ibid., p. 71.

It is through our faith that we receive God's love in our hearts, "for faith unfeigned in Christ's blood causeth thee to love for Christ's sake; which love is the pure love only and the only cause of a good conscience."[1] But God's love stretches beyond us, for it is not only a Father's love to his child, but also something that reaches, through us, to our fellow Christians.

> If we love God for the pleasures that we receive, then love we ourselves. But if we love him to do him pleasure again; that can we no otherwise do, than in loving our neighbours for his sake; them that are good, to continue them in their goodness; and them that are evil, to draw them to good. Love is the instrument wherewith faith maketh us God's sons, and fashioneth us like the image of God, and certifieth us that we so are. And therefore commandeth Christ, "Love your enemies, bless them that curse you, pray for them that persecute you, that ye may be the sons of your heavenly Father; which maketh his sun rise over good and bad, and sendeth his rain upon just and unjust:" yea, which made the sun of his mercy shine upon us, and sent the rain of the blood of his dear and only child upon our souls to quicken us, and to make us see love, to love again.[2]

In our baptism, we made our vows to God, and as we will see when discussing the sacraments, Tyndale constantly reminds us of the importance of keeping the profession of our baptism. However, there were those who said that the Christian should not make vows:

> Thou wilt ask me, Shall I vow nothing at all? Yes, God's commandment, which thou hast vowed in thy baptism. For what intent? Verily, for the love of Christ which hath bought thee with his blood, and made thee son and heir of God with him, that thou shouldst wait on his will and commandments, and purify thy members according to the same doctrine that hath purified thine heart.[3]

As God's child, and part of God's family, the Christian does good works, not for anything he has gained from it, but because he has been called, "and also came unto the marriage, which God the Father made between Christ his Son and all sinners," and who "brought their marriage-garment with them; that is to wit, true faith, wherewith we be married unto Christ, and made his flesh and his blood, and one spirit with him, his brethren and heirs with him, and the sons of God also."[4]

God's child has to learn, and the preacher has the task of teaching, "and

---

1. William Tyndale, *Prologue Matthew, PS-1*, p. 475.
2. William Tyndale, *Exposition 1 John, PS-2*, p. 200.
3. William Tyndale, *Prologue Numbers, PS-1*, p. 433.
4. William Tyndale, *Answer, PS-3*, p. 69.

sheweth them the testament in Christ's blood; how that for his sake all that is done is forgiven, and all their weakness shall be taken a worth, until they be stronger, only if they repent, and will submit themselves to be scholars, and learn to keep this law."[1]

"When the peace is made between God and us, and all forgiven through faith in Christ's blood, and we begin to love the law, we were never the nearer except faith went with us, to supply the lack of full love."[2] For, as with every aspect of our Christian life, our love depends on faith. "For faith unfeigned in Christ's blood causeth thee to love for Christ's sake; which love is the pure love only and the only cause of a good conscience."[3] That faith, as we have seen, is a gift of God (Acts 10:45), and we are dependent for our Christian life on God's love for us as he empowers us to be God's children and to live according to his will. For, "As Paul saith that we are bought with Christ's blood, and therefore are his servants, and not our own, and ought to seek his will and honour only, and to love and serve one another for his sake."[4]

One of the signs that the Christian is a child of God is found in his obedience to God's command: "Hear O Israel: the Lord our God is one Lord: and thou shalt love the Lord thy God with all thine heart, and with all thy soul, and with all thy might." (Deut. 6:5). "Thou shalt love thy neighbour as thyself." (Lev. 19:18).[5] Tyndale felt these commands showed that one was a child of God, a child who was totally dependent on the Trinity for all his needs and for his ability to serve God. When we find people who say that it is our faith that enables us to respond to the gospel and find acceptance by God to be saved and be born again, Tyndale tells us that we have to correct them, and "say thou with Paul, (Rom. vi.) that 'everlasting life is the gift of God through Jesus Christ our Lord.'"[6] For, as we saw earlier in this chapter, faith is not our own,

> but right faith is a thing wrought by the Holy Ghost in us, which changeth us, turneth us into a new nature, and begetteth us anew in God and maketh us the sons of God, as thou readest in the first of John; and killeth the old Adam, and maketh us altogether new in the heart, mind, will, lust, and in all our affections and powers of the soul; the Holy Ghost ever accompanying her, and ruling the heart.[7]

For our salvation is not in our power to choose or attain.

Neither can actual sin be washed away with our works, but with

---

1. Ibid., p. 108f.
2. Ibid., p. 205.
3. William Tyndale, *Prologue, Matthew, PS-1*, p. 475.
4. William Tyndale, *Prologue, Deuteronomy, PS-1*, p. 442.
5. Quoted in the New Testament, Lk. 10:26, 27.
6. William Tyndale, *Prologue Jonas, PS-1*, p. 466.
7. William Tyndale, *Prologue Romans, PS-1*, p. 493.

Christ's blood; neither can there be any other sacrifice, or satisfaction to Godward for them, save Christ's blood: forasmuch as we can do no works unto God, but receive only of his mercy with our repenting faith, through Jesus Christ our Lord and only Saviour: unto whom, and unto God our Father through him, and unto his Holy Spirit, that only purgeth, sanctifieth, and washeth us in the innocent blood of our redemption, be praise for ever. Amen.[1]

However, we are not automatons, for God has restored to us the free will man lost when he first disobeyed God. "We affirm that we have no free will to prevent [go before] God and his grace, and before grace prepare ourselves thereunto; neither can we consent unto God before grace be come. For until God hath prevented [gone before] us, and poured the Spirit of his grace into our souls, to love his laws";[2] giving us a will that is free to choose what is good, and to love God and obey him. "Set thou before thee how that Christ's blood-shedding hath bound us to love one another with all our might, and to do the uttermost in our power one to another.[3] "For the love of a man's neighbour unfeignedly springeth out of the unfeigned knowledge of God in Christ's blood: by which knowledge we be born of God, and love God and our neighbours for his sake."[4]

Finally, the child of God does good works that are pleasing to God, but even these he is unable to call his own and expect God to place a value on them. Therefore, Tyndale wrote that as the child of God, struggles to love God with all his heart, soul, strength and mind,

thy spirit sigheth, mourneth, and longeth after strength to do it, take a sign and evident token thereby, that the Spirit of life is in thee, and that thou art elect to life everlasting by Christ's blood, whose gift and purchase is thy faith, and that Spirit that worketh the will of God in thee; whose gift also are thy deeds, or rather the deeds of the Spirit of Christ, and not thine; and whose gift is the reward of eternal life, which followeth good works.[5]

Thus, we see that man's salvation depends solely upon God. Only the Trinitarian covenant between the three Persons of the Godhead enables man to be set free from Satan's power. Man's salvation is the work of the Holy Spirit, as he sprinkles Christ's blood on God's elect, thus making them a new creation. The elect are thus born anew as children of God and know God as their most loving heavenly Father.

---

1. William Tyndale, *Prologue Jonas, PS-1*, p. 466.
2. William Tyndale, *Answer, PS-3*, p. 174.
3. William Tyndale, *Obedience, PS-1*, p. 329.
4. William Tyndale, *Exposition, 1 John, PS-2*, p. 198.
5. William Tyndale, *Mammon, PS-1*, p. 85.

5. The Christian Life, Worship and the Sacraments

The Christian Life

Moving on from our salvation, the blood of Christ is very important for the Christian's ability to live as a child of God. In fact, the whole of our life has to be lived in obedience to God's laws and commandments as the Holy Spirit sprinkles Christ's blood on us, enabling us to know and obey God's will. However, this does not take away from us our freedom of choice; rather this gives us the power to choose what is good and to make decisions about what path we intend to take in our life's journey.

> Whatsoever is our own is sin. Whatsoever is above that, is Christ's gift, purchase, doing, and working. Whatsoever good thing is in us, that is given us freely, without our deserving or merits, for Christ's blood sake. That we desire to follow the will of God, it is the gift of Christ's blood. That we now hate the devil's will (whereunto we were so fast locked, and could not but love it), is also the gift of Christ's blood; unto whom belongeth the praise and honour of our good deeds and not unto us.[1]

As Christians, we face several challenges in our journey through life – some of these are common to all Christians and others may only be applicable to a few. But it is through the blood of Christ that we are helped in every step that we take.

The Christian's journey is completely varied; there are times when everything seems to be going so smoothly that it seems that nothing can go wrong, almost as if we have overcome the temptations that we once faced. Then suddenly, when we are least prepared for it, Satan attacks us, so subtly that we are hardly able to recognise the temptation. He also will remind us of the sins that we found hardest to overcome in our life and often of the sins that we enjoyed in our childhood. Then, the Christian

---

1. William Tyndale, *1525, New Testament*, p. 14.

mourneth in his heart because he is in such bondage that he cannot do the will of God; and is an hungred and athirst after righteousness; for righteousness (I mean) which springeth out of Christ's blood, for strength to do the will of God; and turneth him to the promises of God, and desireth him for his great mercy and truth, and for the blood of his Son Christ, to fulfil his promises, and to give him strength.[1]

But it is not in the Christian's power to overcome these temptations of Satan in his own strength; he needs God's help. "And God hath bound himself, that if I come in the right way, by the door of Christ's blood, and ask help, that he will send me, if need be, an hundred legions of angels or saints"[2] Help does not automatically come for us; we must seek God our Father in our prayers with the awareness that he has promised to hear us when we pray in faith.

It is when God has answered our prayer of faith and dealt with these temptations that we realise afresh that "faith in Christ's blood (which is God's promise) quieteth the conscience of the true believers".[3] It is then that we realise all that God has done for us; that

In Christ's blood are we blessed from that bitter curse and damnable captivity under sin, wherein we were born and conceived. And Christ's Spirit is poured into us, to bring forth good works, and our works are the fruits of the Spirit; and the kingdom is the deserving of Christ's blood, and so is faith, and the Spirit, and good works also.[4]

As Christians, we are not alone in our journey through life, but, as our life closely copies the life of Christ, Christ's blood unites us with others who are sharing the journey. "If ye counterfeit and follow God in well doing, then no doubt it is a sign that the Spirit of God is in you, and also the favour of God, which is not in the world; and that ye are inheritors of all the promises of God, and elect unto the fellowship of the blood of Christ."[5] However, this is not easy for us to achieve. It is easy for us to take pride in our 'goodness' and think that the things we do assure us of God's approval. "He that seeketh with his alms *more than* to be merciful to a neighbour, . . . the same is blind, and seeth not what it is to be a Christian man, and to have fellowship in Christ's blood"[6] (italics mine). For then we have not realised that, however much we have done, we have failed to reach the standard

---

1. William Tyndale, *Mammon, PS-1*, p. 75.
2. William Tyndale, *Exposition 1 John, PS-2*, p. 167.
3. William Tyndale, *Exposition Matthew, PS-2*, p. 11.
4. William Tyndale, *Mammon, PS-1*, p. 83.
5. Ibid., p. 72.
6. Ibid., p. 100.

Christ showed us. The compassion we show to our neighbours reflects that "compassion and love spring of the love we have to God in Christ, for the pure mercy and love that he hath shewed on us: then have we a sure token that we are beloved of God, and washed in Christ's blood, and elect, by Christ's deserving, unto eternal life".[1]

Tyndale wrote an exposition on the Sermon on the Mount,[2] and he believed that the beatitudes are important for teaching us about our Christian life. In his *1525, New Testament*, he had an important note about them.

> All these deeds here rehearsed as to nourish peace, to show mercy, to suffer persecution, and so forth, make not a man happy and blessed, neither deserve the reward of heaven: but declare and testify that we are happy and blessed, and that we shall have great promotion in heaven, and certifieth us in our hearts that we are God's sons, and that the Holy Ghost is in us. For all good things are given to us freely of God for Christ's blood's sake and his merits.[3]

Tyndale took over 15 pages in his *Exposition upon the Fifth, Sixth, and Seventh of Matthew* to explain the beatitudes, and he draws our attention to the blessings that God gives us as we follow in his path as a child of God. But he also warns us of the dangers that confront man if he follows the ways of those who are going the ways of the fallen man.

The Church

One of the signs that we have been born again and are alive as God's children is through being members of God's family, when the blessings of the beatitudes are found in our life. Then, as children of God we all meet together to show that God created us to have fellowship with our brothers and sisters in our Father's house, and so churches were built so that we could gather as the disciples round the Lord's table to worship God.

At the beginning of his *Answer to Sir Thomas More's Dialogue*, Tyndale describes different meanings of the word 'church'. "Throughout all the scripture, the church is taken for the whole multitude of them that believe in Christ in that place, in that parish, town, city, province, land, or throughout all the world." Tyndale continues: "Notwithstanding yet it is sometimes taken generally for all of them that embrace the name of Christ, though their faiths be nought, or though they have no faith at all. And sometimes it is

---

1. Ibid., p. 107.
2. William Tyndale, *An Exposition uppon the v. vi. vii. Chapters of Mathew, PS-2*, pp. 3–132.
3. William Tyndale, *1525, New Testament*, p. 23, marginal note to Mt. 5:3–12.

taken specially for the elect only."[1] It is with the elect that we are concerned, rather than any of the other meanings of the church. The elect are few and are therefore called a 'little flock'. "The kingdom of heaven is the preaching of the gospel, unto which come both good and bad. But the good are few. Christ calleth them therefore a 'little flock,' Luke xii."[2] Tyndale expands on this idea:

> But little flock, as soon as he is persuaded that there is a God, he runneth not unto his own imaginations, but unto the messenger that called him, and of him asketh how he shall serve God. . . . And the preacher setteth the law of God before them; and they offer their hearts, to have it written therein, consenting that it is good and righteous. And because they have run clean contrary unto that good law, they sorrow and mourn; and because, also, their bodies and flesh are otherwise disposed. But the preacher comforteth them, and sheweth them the testament of Christ's blood; how that for his sake all that is done is forgiven, and all their weakness shall be taken a worth, until they be stronger, only if they repent, and will submit themselves to be scholars, and learn to keep this law. And little flock receiveth this testament in his heart, and in it walketh and serveth God in the spirit.[3]

It is in the fellowship of the Church that God's children meet, and their faith is strengthened as they join together with God their Father and with one another, and to share together the family meal of the Lord's Supper.

Worship

Tyndale is of the view that worship is to be found not so much in church services and our prayers but in the way we live in obedience to God's commandments. For only when we realise our sin and God's love and power to set us free from our sin, we are drawn by the Holy Spirit to love and worship God.

> For whosoever feeleth the just damnation of sin, and the forgiveness and mercy that is in Christ's blood for all that repent and forsake it, and come and believe in that mercy, the same only knoweth how God is to be honoured and worshipped, and can judge between true serving of God in the spirit, and false image-serving of God with works. And the same knoweth that sacraments, signs, ceremonies, and bodily things can be no service to God in his person; but memorials unto men, and a remembrance of the testament, wherewith God is served in the spirit.[4]

1. William Tyndale, *Answer, PS-3*, p. 13.
2. William Tyndale, *Obedience, PS-1*, p. 165.
3. William Tyndale, *Answer, PS-3*, p. 108f.
4. Ibid., p. 56.

As we love the Lord our God with all our heart, soul, mind and strength, our new life of worship will be revealed through our lives.

God's worship is to love him for his mercy; and of love to bestow all our works upon our neighbour for his sake, and upon the taming of our flesh, that we sin not again, which should be the chiefest care of a christian man; whilst Christ careth for that that is once past and committed already, whether before our profession or after. For the conditions of the peace that is made between God and us in Christ's blood are these: The law is set before us, unto which if we consent and submit ourselves to be scholars thereof, then are not only all our fore sins forgiven, both *pœna et culpa* (with our holy father's licence ever); but also all our infirmities, weakness, proneness, readiness, and motions unto sin, are pardoned, and taken a worth.[1]

Tyndale says that our sins are forgiven, our tendency to fall when tempted is pardoned and we are enabled to keep our profession of faith, which we made when we were baptised. For it is through loving our neighbour as ourselves that we show we love God with heart, soul, mind and strength, and it is through loving God that we worship God. So, Tyndale tells us to "understand that the words which the scripture useth, in the worshipping or honouring of God, are these: Love God, cleave to God, dread, serve, bow, pray, and call on God, believe and trust in God, and such like".[2]

Worship is something that is within man, for

The temple wherein God will be worshipped, is the heart of man. For 'God is a Spirit' (saith Christ, John iv.), 'and will be worshipped in the spirit and in truth:' that is, when a penitent heart consenteth unto the law of God, and with a strong faith longeth for the promises of God. So is God honoured on all sides, in that we count him righteous in all his laws and ordinances, and also trust in all his promises. Other worshipping of God is there none, except we make an idol of him."[3]

Prayer

One of the many ways by which our worship of God is revealed is through our prayers. Although Tyndale teaches different aspects of prayer in his writings, his doctrine of Christ's blood has a more limited place in our prayers.

For first, God, which alone hath power to help or hurt, hath made

---

1. William Tyndale, *Exposition 1 John, PS-2*, p. 158.
2. William Tyndale, *Answer, PS-3*, p. 57.
3. William Tyndale, *Mammon, PS-1*, p. 106.

appointment betwixt him and us, in Christ's blood; and hath bound himself to give us whatsoever we ask in his name, testifying thereto that there is no other name to be saved by; and that he will be a father unto us, and save us both in this life and in the life to come, and take us from under the damnation of the law, and set us under grace and mercy, to be scholars only to learn the law.[1]

God's promise is to "give us whatsoever we ask in his name" and open up to us the power of prayer in our Christian life.

There are only two areas of prayer where Tyndale mentions the importance of the blood of Christ, both of which concern our need for help. The first of these concerns the help we can expect from God when we pray to him through our faith in Christ's blood.

If my faith be stedfast in the promises that I have in Christ's blood, I need but pray my Father in Christ's name, and he shall send me a legion of angels to help me; so that my faith is lord over the angels, and over all creatures, to turn them unto my soul's health and my father's honour, and may be subject unto no creature, but unto God's word in our Saviour Christ only.[2]

The second concerns asking other people to pray for us. Tyndale had condemned the Catholic practice of praying to saints, for them to be mediators between God and us. Also their practice of prayers for the dead, because they thought that these prayers could positively open the door to God, and they, as mediators, cause God to answer the petition. William Tracy, in his will, had written,

My ground and my belief is, that there is but one God, and one mediator between God and man, which is Jesus Christ: so that I do accept none in heaven, nor in earth, to be my mediator between me and God, but only Jesus Christ; all other be but petitioners in receiving of grace, but none able to give influence of grace.[3]

Tyndale, in his *Exposition of Tracy's Testament*, commented on this statement,

That he excludeth, in that he saith all others be but petitioners: by which words he plainly confesseth, that other may and ought for to pray, and that we may and ought to desire other to pray for us; but meaneth that we may not put our trust and confidence in their prayer, as though they gave of themselves that which they desire for us in their

---

1. William Tyndale, *Exposition 1 John, PS-2*, p. 166.
2. William Tyndale, *Answer, PS-3*, p. 116f.
3. William Tyndale, *Tracy, PS-3*, p. 272.

petitions, and so give them the thanks, and ascribe to their merits that which is given us in the name of our master Christ, as the deservings of his blood.[1]

Tyndale, in *Obedience*, commented on the importance of praying for others, "To pray one for another are we equally bound, and to pray is a thing that we may always do, whatsoever we have in hand; and that to do may no man hire another, Christ's blood hath hired us already."[2]

Tyndale believed that our prayers cannot be limited to a specific time or place, and so, commenting on Matthew 7:7-11, he wrote,

> First, note of these words, that to pray is God's commandment, as it is to believe in God, to love God, or to love thy neighbour; and so are alms and fasting also. Neither is it possible to believe in God, to love him, or to love thy neighbour, but that prayer will spring out there-hence immediately. For to believe in God is to be sure that all thou hast is of him, and all thou needest must come of him: which if thou do, thou canst not but continually thank him for his benefits, which thou continually, without ceasing, receivest of his hand; and thereto ever cry for help, for thou art ever in need, and canst no whence else be holpen.[3]

We now pass onto another important aspect of our prayers, which is thanking God for all his mercies to us.

Thanksgiving

The Papal Church claimed that the saints had done more good works than God required of them, and so the excess 'good works' could be passed on to others, and in this way to bring forgiveness to those who had fallen short of God's requirements. Tyndale contradicted this idea, and wrote,

> When we have sinned, we go with a repenting heart unto Christ's blood, and there wash it off through faith. And our deeds are but thanksgiving to God, to help our neighbours at their need, for which our neighbours and each of them owe us as much again at our need. So that the testament, or forgiveness of sins, is built upon faith in Christ's blood, and not on works.[4]

Thanking God for the answers he gives to our prayers is important, and we must never take them for granted. We must thank God for the forgiveness of our sins. We must thank God when he has answered our prayers. We must

1. Ibid., p. 277f.
2. William Tyndale, *Obedience, PS-1*, p. 280.
3. William Tyndale, *Exposition Matthew, PS-2*, p. 115.
4. William Tyndale, *Answer, PS-3*, p. 204.

thank God for the prayers others have made for us, or we for them. For we must follow the example of William Tracy, who, "trusting faithfully to his promise; thanking, as ye may see by his words, the blood of Christ for the reward promised to his works, and not the goodness of the works, as though he had done more than his duty."[1]

Teaching and Preaching

The spiritualty taught the people all kinds of errors, through which the Papal Church amassed its wealth and impoverished the laity; Tyndale condemned them for their rejection of God's teaching and for leading the laity astray from a true faith in God's love.

> Yet, if they had been as loving, kind, careful and diligent to teach the people to repent, and to believe in the blood of Christ for the forgiveness of their sins, unto the glory and mercy of God, and of his exceeding love to us, and unto the profit of our souls; and, upon that preaching, to have ministered the sacrament as a memorial, remembrance, . . . for the assurance of the promise of God; to quiet, stablish and certify our consciences, and to put us out of all wavering and doubt, that our sins were forgiven us, and God become our father and at one with us, for which cause only Christ ordained it.[2]

The sermon is an important part of our worship, and through preaching, the worshipper is taught the truth and the reason behind the acts of worship of God's children.

Tyndale followed the Wycliffites, and also Erasmus, in writing about true and false teachers; Tyndale criticised the friars and monks who went around preaching to the people. They were false preachers, for

> these are enemies unto the cross of Christ, and preach their belly, which is their God, . . . and they think that lucre is the serving of God: . . . Their longing is to fill their paunch, whom they serve, and not Christ; and through sweet preaching, and flattering words, deceive the hearts of the simple and unlearned. A true preacher preacheth Christ's testament only; and maketh Christ the cause and reward of all our deeds; and teacheth every man to bear his cross willingly for Christ's sake.[3]

Tyndale gives the structure of Paul's epistles as an example to the preacher:

---

1. William Tyndale, *Tracy, PS-3*, p. 280.
2. William Tyndale, *Exposition 1 John, PS-2*, p. 222.
3. William Tyndale, *Obedience, PS-1*, p. 300.

First, he preacheth the law, and proveth that the whole nature of man is damned, in that the heart lusteth contrary to the will of God. For if we were of God, no doubt we should have lust in his will. Then preacheth he Christ, the gospel, the promises, and the mercy that God hath set forth to all men in Christ's blood: which they that believe, and take it for an earnest thing, turn themselves to God, begin to love God again, and to prepare themselves to his will, by the working of the Spirit of God in them. Last of all, exhorteth he to unity, peace and soberness, to avoid brawlings, sects, opinions, disputing and arguing about words; and to walk in the plain and single faith and feeling of the Spirit; and to love one another after the ensample of Christ, even as Christ loved us; and to be thankful and to walk worthy of the gospel, and as it becometh Christ; and with the ensample of pure living to draw all to Christ.[1]

Of course, Tyndale would not expect every sermon to cover every point that Paul listed in his epistles, but sermons should cover the ground that Christians needed to know if they were to live a full, spiritual Christian life. He wrote of the need that those people had, who only knew the preaching of the friars and secular clergy, who were false preachers whose sermons were confined to the teaching of the pope's Church; however,

When a true preacher preacheth, the Spirit entereth the hearts of the elect, and maketh them feel the righteousness of the law of God, and by the law the poison of their corrupt nature; and thence leadeth them, through repentance, unto the mercy that is in Christ's blood; and as an ointment healeth the body, even so the Spirit, through confidence and trust in Christ's blood, healeth the soul, and maketh her love the law of God.[2]

Tyndale then mentions the dangers that a preacher faces, dangers that can lead him astray and weaken his message.

If the preacher which for his doctrine is called salt, have lost the nature of salt, that is to say, his sharpness in rebuking all unrighteousness, all natural reason, natural wit and understanding, and all trust and confidence in whatsoever it be, save in the blood of Christ; he is condemned of God, and disallowed of all them that cleave to the truth.[3]

The Sacraments

Tyndale, like most of the Reformers, only accepted Baptism and the Lord's Supper as sacraments. I have shown in my book, *The Theology of William Tyndale*, Tyndale's views on the five other sacraments of the Roman Catholic

---

1. William Tyndale, *Mammon, PS-1*, p. 96f.
2. William Tyndale, *Exposition 1 John, PS-2*, p. 183f.
3. William Tyndale, *Exposition Matthew, PS-2*, p. 33.

Church. Tyndale disagreed with Luther over Confession, for Luther wrote in *The Large Catechism*, "when I exhort you to go to confession, I am doing nothing but exhorting you to be a Christian."[1] Thomas More wrote, "Tyndale saith that confession is the worst invention that ever was." Tyndale replied, "As ye fashion it, mean I, and of that filthy Priapish confession, which ye spew in the ear; wherewith ye exclude the forgiveness that is in Christ's blood, for all that repent and believe therein; and make the people believe that their sins be never forgiven until they be shriven unto the priest."[2]

Tyndale believed that the law of Moses could be divided into three parts. First, signs by which we remember what God has done for us; second, signs that remind us of God's promises and his covenant with man and third, sacrifices by which God forgave the sins of man.

> Part of his laws are ceremonies, that is to say, signs that put men in remembrance either of the benefits of God done already, as the Easter lamb; either signs of the promise and appointment made between God and man, as circumcision; or signs that testify unto the people that the wrath of God is peaced, and their sins forgiven, as all manner sacrifices: which all ceased as soon as Christ had offered up the sacrifice of his body and blood for us; and instead of them come the open preaching of Christ, and our signs which we call sacraments.[3]

In his exposition of 1 John 5:5 about sacraments being witnesses to us, Tyndale wrote,

> Christ came with three witnesses, water, blood, and Spirit. He ordained the sacrament of baptism, to be his witness unto us. And he ordained the sacrament of his blood, to be his witness unto us. And he poureth his Spirit into the hearts of his, to testify and to make them feel that the testimony of those two sacraments are true. And the testimony of these three is, as it after followeth, that we have everlasting life in the Son of God.[4]

We will consider the two sacraments that Tyndale accepted, but only where Tyndale mentioned them in his doctrine of the blood of Christ. Because the Lord's Supper depends on Christ's blood in a sacramental way, we will also consider those passages where Tyndale's use of 'the blood of Christ' relates to our Christian life, and not to its sacramental role.

Tyndale believed that there was a continuity between the Old and the New Testaments, the blood of the sacrifices in the Old Testament represented the blood of Christ that was, at a later date, to be shed. Therefore, the Old Testament sacraments were continued into the New Testament up to the end

1. Martin Luther, *Book of Concord*, p. 479.
2. William Tyndale, *Answer, PS-3*, p. 171f.
3. William Tyndale, *Prelates, PS-2*, p. 324.
4. William Tyndale, *Exposition 1 John, PS-2*, p. 209f.

of Christ's earthly ministry, but after Christ's blood had been shed, there was to be no more sacrifices of blood offered to God. This meant that the human blood shed in Circumcision was replaced by the water in Baptism, and the lamb's blood shed in the Passover meal was replaced by wine in the Lord's Supper. All the other Old Testament sacrifices were not sacramental, but related to the many different ways by which Christ's blood affects the Christian's life as a child of God.

There are certain things that are common to all sacraments; they must have a signification, and they must also preach Christ to us, otherwise they condemn our Christian faith. Tyndale believed that, apart from Baptism and the Lord's Supper, the five other sacraments of the Roman Church were a false invention of the papacy and are all without signification.

> Wherefore, inasmuch as the sacraments of the Old Testament have significations; and inasmuch as the sacraments of the New Testament (of which mention is made that they were delivered unto us by the very apostles, at Christ's commandment) have also significations; and inasmuch as the office of an apostle is to edify in Christ; and inasmuch as a dumb ceremony edifieth not, but hurteth altogether (for if it preach not unto me, then I cannot but put confidence therein that the deed justfieth me, which is the denying of Christ's blood); and inasmuch as no mention is made of them, as well as of other, nor is known what is meant by them; therefore it appeareth that the apostles taught them not, but that they be the false merchandise of wily hypocrites.[1]

As we have seen, the sacrament also preaches to us the gospel.

> *More:* – "He teacheth that the sacrament hath no virtue at all, but the faith only." *Tyndale* – The faith of a repenting soul in Christ's blood doth justify only. And the sacrament standeth in as good stead as a lively preacher. And as the preacher justifieth me not, but my faith in the doctrine; even so the sign justifieth not, but the faith in the promise, which the sacrament signifieth and preacheth.[2]

In fact, those who thought that the sacrament in itself conveyed the grace of God, were misled,

> as they which pray to God in the sacrament not only do, but also through that opinion, as they have lost love to their neighbours, even so have they lost the true faith in the covenant made in Christ's blood and body: which covenant only is that which saveth. And to testify this, was the sacrament instituted only.[3]

1. William Tyndale, *Answer, PS-3*, p. 29.
2. Ibid., p. 172 (see *CWM-6*, p. 352).
3. William Tyndale, *Sacraments, PS-1*, p. 385.

Baptism and Circumcision

God gave Abraham the sacrament of circumcision, and the blood shed in that sacrament made the link between the child and God, and this blood pointed to the time when Christ's blood would be shed. After Christ had shed his blood on the Cross, circumcision ceased and was replaced by water in baptism.

> By baptism we are bound to God, and God to us, and the bond and seal of the covenant is written in our flesh; by which seal or writing God challengeth faith and love, under pain of just damnation: and we (if we believe and love) challenge (as it is above rehearsed) all mercy, and whatsoever we need; or else God must be an untrue God. And God hath bound us christian men to receive this sign for our infirmities' sake, to be a witness between him and us, and also to put this sign upon our children; . . . to bring them to the knowledge of God the Father, and of Christ, and of their duty to God and his law. And as the circumcised in the flesh, and not in the heart, have no part in God's good promises; even so they that be baptized in the flesh, and not in heart, have no part in Christ's blood.[1]

That quotation from Tyndale's *Treatise* on the *Sacrament of Baptism and on the Lord's Supper* covers much of the ground behind Tyndale's theology of the sealing of the covenant between God and his chosen people, both before and after Christ's death and resurrection.

> The covenant made between God and Abraham, saved the man-child as soon as it was born, yea, as soon as it had life in the mother's womb: for the covenant, that God would be God of Abraham's seed, went over the fruit as soon as it had life; . . . even so must needs the covenant, made to all that believe in Christ's blood, go over that seed as soon as it hath life in the mother's womb, before the sign be put on it. For it is the covenant only, and not the sign, that saveth us; though the sign be commanded to be put on at due time, to stir up faith of the covenant that saveth us. And instead of circumcision came our baptism; whereby we be received into the religion of Christ, and made partakers of his passion, and members of his church.[2]

Tyndale links circumcision and baptism very clearly in his 'Table expounding certain words in Genesis'.

> TESTAMENT: that is, an appointment made between God and man, and God's promises. And sacrament is a sign representing such

---

1. Ibid., p. 350f.
2. Ibid., p. 350.

appointment and promises. . . . And circumcision representeth the promises of God to Abraham, on the one side; and that Abraham and his seed should circumcise, and cut off the lusts of their flesh, on the other side, to walk in the ways of the Lord: as baptism, which is come in the room thereof, now signifieth on the one side, how that all that repent and believe are washed in Christ's blood; and on the other side, how that the same must quench and drown the lusts of the flesh, to follow the steps of Christ.[1]

Also, in his *Prologue to the Book of Leviticus*, Tyndale wrote,

And as circumcision was a token certifying them that they were received unto the favour of God, and their sins forgiven them; even so baptism certifieth us that we are washed in the blood of Christ, and received to favour for his sake: and as circumcision signifieth unto them the cutting away of their own lusts, and slaying of their free-will, as they call it, to follow the will of God; even so baptism signifieth unto us repentance, and the mortifying of our unruly members and body of sin, to walk in a new life, and so forth.[2]

Tyndale disagreed with the Roman Catholic teaching that the Holy Spirit was in the water; therefore, the act of baptism in itself saved the person baptised. In a marginal note, he wrote, "Not naked or dumb ceremonies, but the Holy Ghost, through faith, washeth away sins."[3] Tyndale sent those who believed that the act of baptism was all that was needed to Paul,

which asked his Galatians, whether they received the Holy Ghost by the deed of the law, or by preaching of faith; and there concludeth that the Holy Ghost accompanieth the preaching of faith. . . . So now if baptism preach me the washing in Christ's blood, so doth the Holy Ghost accompany it; and that deed of preaching through faith doth put away my sins.[4]

The important thing about one's baptism are the promises made to God by the person baptised, and Tyndale frequently reminds his readers of the importance of their baptismal promises, usually without making any reference to Christ's blood. Although in his *Exposition of the First Epistle of St. John*, Tyndale wrote,

And to have this profession written in thine heart is to consent unto the law that it is righteous and good, and to love it in thine heart,

1. William Tyndale, *1530, Old Testament, PS-1*, p. 409.
2. William Tyndale, *Prologue to Leviticus, PS-1*, p. 426.
3. Ibid. p. 424.
4. Ibid.

and to submit thyself thereto for to learn it, and to rule and square all thy deeds thereby; and then to believe in Christ, that for his sake all thy sins, which thou didst before the knowledge of this profession, are forgiven thee clearly, . . . and that for none other satisfaction to Godward than Christ's blood.[1]

Because of the link between circumcision for God's people before Christ's blood was shed and baptism after the crucifixion, Tyndale firmly believed in infant baptism. Therefore, Tyndale could write,

> though when we sin of frailty after our baptism, we receive the sign no more, yet we be renewed again through repentance, and faith in Christ's blood; of which twain that sign of baptism, ever continued among us in baptizing our young children, doth ever keep us in mind, and call us back again unto our profession, if we be gone astray, and promiseth us forgiveness. Neither can actual sin be washed away with our works, but with Christ's blood; neither can there be any other sacrifice, or satisfaction to Godward for them, save Christ's blood: forasmuch as we can do no works unto God, but receive only of his mercy with our repenting faith, through Jesus Christ our Lord and only Saviour: unto whom, and unto God our Father through him, and unto his Holy Spirit, that only purgeth, sanctifieth, and washeth us in the innocent blood of our redemption be praise for ever.[2]

Because Tyndale believed in infant baptism, he believed that the promises made when a child was baptised had to be confirmed when the child was old enough to know what they meant. Confirmation was not a sacrament, and because it did not affect the child as a Christian, the blood of Christ was not a part of this ceremony. However, Tyndale believed that before a child could confirm its baptismal promises (made for it by his godparents), it had to be taught the Christian faith and the meaning of the promises that it was going to confirm from the age of 6 or 7 until about 14 and to take personal responsibility to keep its promises to God.[3]

Lord's Supper and the Passover

As with Baptism and Circumcision, Tyndale said that the Old Testament sacrament of the Passover had the same meaning as the Lord's Supper. The difference was that in the pre-Christian sacrament, a lamb shed its blood, and the Israelites fed on that lamb in remembrance of their being freed from

---

1. William Tyndale, *Exposition 1 John, PS-2*, p. 136f.
2. William Tyndale, *Prologue Jonas, PS-1*, p. 466.
3. William Tyndale, *Answer, PS-3*, p. 71f; *Obedience, PS-1*, p. 273.

slavery to Pharaoh, in order to serve God. For the Christian sacrament, Christ, the Lamb of God, shed his blood on the Cross, and since Christ's flesh could not be eaten, bread was substituted for it. Christians feed on this bread, signifying their freedom from slavery to the Devil, in order that they can serve God.

> And (Exod, xii.) God gave the children of Israel the sign of Pesah, which we call the Easter Lamb, for a sign that the time was come that the children of Israel should be delivered out of Egypt. . . . and to deliver them, he commanded them to take for every house a lamb or a kid, and to slay them, and to strike the door-posts with the blood, to be a sign to them, and a seal of the promise that God would deliver them that night both out of the hands of Pharao, and also from the smiting of the angel that went about all Egypt, and slew the first-born in every house. And this sign Pesah, beside that it was a seal of the promise to be delivered the same night, to stablish that faith, and commanded to be observed ever after yearly, to keep the benefit in memory; it was also a very prophecy of the passion of Christ, describing the very manner and fashion of his death, and the effect and virtue thereof also. In whose stead is the sacrament of the body and blood of Christ come, as baptism in the room or stead of circumcision.[1]

Contrary to the teaching of the papal Church, Tyndale clearly separated the Lord's Supper from the idea that it was a sacrifice.

> If a man say of the sacrament of Christ's body and blood, that it is a sacrifice as well for the dead as for the quick, and therefore the very deed itself justifieth and putteth away sin; I answer, that a sacrifice is the slaying of the body of a beast, or a man: wherefore, if it be a sacrifice, then is Christ's body there slain, and his blood there shed; but that is not so. And therefore it is properly no sacrifice, but a sacrament, and a memorial of that everlasting sacrifice once for all, which he offered upon the cross now upon a fifteen hundred years ago; and preacheth only unto them that are alive.[2]

God knows how easy it is for man to forget things and perhaps just repeat actions without understanding the reason for them. As a boy, I remember why we celebrated 5 November, because Guy Fawkes was prevented from blowing up the House of Parliament and killing the king and members of the Lords and Commons; also, I knew why my Roman

---

1. William Tyndale, *Sacraments, PS-1*, p. 353f.
2. William Tyndale, *Prologue Leviticus, PS-1*, p. 424.

Catholic friends were not allowed to celebrate it. Now, the reason for the Gunpowder Plot has been forgotten. Christ told his disciples to keep the Lord's Supper so that we might remember (and never forget) the cost of our salvation. He said "This do in remembrance of me." Tyndale wrote, "Here ye see by these words, that it was ordained to keep the death of Christ in mind, and to testify that his body was given and his blood shed for us." Tyndale quotes Christ's words from another account of the Last Supper, and writes, "Lo, here ye see again that it was instituted to keep the death of Christ in mind; and to testify wherefore he died, even to save us from sin, death and hell, that we should seek none other means to be delivered with; for there is none other name for us to be saved by, but only by the name of Jesus."[1]

Signs of Life

Although it is through the blood of Christ that one is made alive and becomes a child of God, there are many aspects in a Christian's life that separate him from those who have not been born anew. Tyndale stresses the two commandments that summarise God's law: that we should love God with the whole of our being, and love our neighbour as we love ourselves.

Love God

Tyndale wrote that the Christian was to "take an ensample in the great commandment, 'Love God with all thine heart:' the spiritual searcheth the cause, and looketh on the benefits of God, and so conceiveth love in heart."[2] There are almost no references to Christ's blood connected to our loving God. However, the Christian's love to God leads the Christian to love God's law, so that

> when the peace is made between God and us, and all forgiven through faith in Christ's blood, and we begin to love the law, we were never the nearer except faith went with us, to supply out the lack of full love; in that we have promises, that that little we have is taken aworth, and accepted till more come.[3]

Loving God leads the Christian to show that love is true by his good works which reach out in love to our neighbour, for without that, our claims to love God are unreal and unsubstantiated.

---

1. William Tyndale, *Sacraments, PS-1*, p. 356.
2. William Tyndale, *Answer, PS-3*, p. 6.
3. William Tyndale, *Answer, PS-3*, p. 205f.

Love thy Neighbour

Tyndale places emphasis on loving our neighbour, for, unless we do, we cannot show that we love God. Tyndale refers to John's lengthy passage on loving our neighbour (1 Jn 4:7-21) in his Exposition:[1]

> John singeth his old song again; and teacheth an infallible and sure token, which we may see and feel at our finger's ends, and thereby be out of all doubt, that our faith is unfeigned, and that we know God, and be born of God, . . . which token is, if we love one another.[2]

Because we are only considering 'the blood of Christ', we will not be considering all that Tyndale teaches about loving our neighbour in this part of his *Exposition*.

> For the love of a man's neighbour unfeignedly springeth out of the unfeigned knowledge of God in Christ's blood: by which knowledge we be born of God, and love God and our neighbours for his sake. And so he that loveth his neighbour unfeignedly is sure of himself, that he knoweth God, and is of God unfeignedly: and contrariwise, he that loveth not, knoweth not God; for God in Christ's blood is such a love, that if a man saw it, it were impossible that he should not break out into the love of God again, and of his neighbour for his sake.[3]

However, this love is not something that comes naturally to man, for John wrote, "Herein is love, not that we loved God, but that he loved us, and sent his Son a satisfaction for our sins." (1 Jn 4:10). This leads us to Tyndale's statement about man after the Fall and to a lengthy exposition on Ephesians 2:1-10 that we were "dead in trespasses and sins." So, without all deservings, without our endeavouring, enforcing and preparing ourselves, and without all good motions, qualities and properties of our free will, we

> beheld with the eyes of a strong faith the mercy, favour and grace, the taking away of the damnation of the law, and restoring again of life, freely offered us in Christ's blood, he should perceive love, and so much the more, that it was shewed us when we were enemies to God."[4]

Tyndale, in his *Answer to Sir Thomas More*, continues this theme:

> And therefore until that love be come, thou must knowledge unfeignedly that there is sin in the best deed thou doest; and it must

1. William Tyndale, *Exposition 1 John, PS-2*, p. 198.
2. Ibid.
3. Ibid.
4. Ibid., p. 199.

earnestly grieve thine heart, and thou must wash all thy good deeds in Christ's blood, ere they can be pure, and an acceptable sacrifice unto God, and must desire God the Father for his sake to take thy deeds a worth, and to pardon the imperfectness of them, and to give thee power to do them better, and with more fervent love.[1]

Therefore, the best deeds that we do to help our neighbours must come from the righteousness that God gives us through the blood of Christ. Only then

we will receive of the merciful kindness of our Father; and will serve our brethren freely of very love; and will be their servants, and suffer for their sakes. And thereto, our good deeds, which we do unto our neighbour's need, spring out of our righteousness or justifying, which is the forgiveness of our sins in Christ's blood; and of other righteousness know we not before God.[2]

It follows, therefore, "If thou have devotion to help thy brother in all his misfortunes, because he is the image of God and price of Christ's blood, then thy devotion certifieth thee that thou art in the favour of God, or state of grace."[3] However, if I break the law, and do not show my love to God through loving my neighbour, "then I dishonour God. . . . If I hurt my neighbour, then I dishonour my neighbour and him that made him, and him also that bought him with his blood."[4]

Good Works

If we have been born anew, the signs of this new life will be seen in our behaviour. This shows itself in the second of God's commandments of love. Tyndale links our ability to do good works with our liberty from our bondage to sin:

In Christ's blood are we blessed from that bitter curse and damnable captivity under sin, wherein we were born and conceived. And Christ's Spirit is poured into us, to bring forth good works, and our works are the fruits of the Spirit; and the kingdom is the deserving of Christ's blood; and so is faith, and the Spirit, and good works also. Notwithstanding the kingdom followeth good works; and good works testify that we are heirs thereof.[5]

---

1. William Tyndale, *Prologue Jonas, PS-1*, p. 463.
2. William Tyndale, *Answer, PS-3*, p. 81f.
3. William Tyndale, *Exposition 1 John, PS-2*, p. 172.
4. William Tyndale, *Answer, PS-3*, p. 58.
5. William Tyndale, *Mammon, PS-1*, p. 83.

"Since I am coupled to God by Christ's blood, do I well, not for heaven's sake, but because I am heir of heaven by grace and Christ's purchasing and have the Spirit of God, I do good freely, for so is my nature."[1]

Tyndale, in his *Exposition of Tracy's Testament*, wrote about the good works that Tracy had done during his lifetime. These had not been done for any reward that God might have given him,

> but patiently abiding for the blessings that God hath appointed unto all manner good works, trusting faithfully to his promise; thanking, as you may see by his words, the blood of Christ for the reward promised to his works, and not the goodness of the works, as though he had done more than his duty, or all that."[2]

"And whensoever an occasion is given, he worketh naturally the will of God: for this blessing is given to all them that trust in Christ's blood, that they thirst and hunger to do God's will."[3]

We see that the change, from being dead in sin, a slave of Satan and an enemy of God, into a Christian, is completely the work of God, without anything in us to deserve God's grace. We are powerless to love God and our neighbour, to worship and serve God, and to do any good works that are pleasing to God: we are only enabled to do all these things by the power of the Holy Spirit as he sprinkles us with the blood of Christ.

---

1. William Tyndale, *1525, New Testament*, p. 14.
2. William Tyndale, *Exposition Tracy's Testament, PS-3*, p. 280.
3. William Tyndale, *Mammon, PS-1*, p. 55.

6. Errors of the Pope's Church

There are a number of instances in which Tyndale explained that the teachings of the pope and the Catholic Church denied the doctrine of the blood of Christ. He drew his readers' attention to the true meaning of the doctrine as it is found in Scripture. It was no wonder that the Church erred and led God's people astray. He wrote about Bishop Tunstal,

> For what service done in Christ's gospel came he to the bishoprick of London; or what such service he did therein? He burnt the New Testament, calling it *Doctrinam peregrinam*, 'strange learning' Yea, verily, look how strange his living in whose blood that testament was made, was from the living of the pope; even so strange is that doctrine from the pope's law."[1]

The pope's Church taught that one of the greatest works that parents could do was to give their children to God, so that the boys became monks, friars or secular clergy, and the girls became nuns. Tyndale criticised this quite strongly;

> First his false doctrine; wherewith the elders beguiled compel their children, and sacrifice them to burn in the pope's chastity, with no other mind than those old idolaters sacrificed their children unto the false god Moloch; so that they think by the merits of their children's burning, after the pope's false doctrine, to please God and to get heaven, clean ignorant of the testament made in Christ's blood.[2]

Thus we see that the parents had been promised God's blessings because they had given their children to serve God in the pope's Church. The children had to promise that they would be chaste and overcome any attractions they might experience to someone of the opposite sex, in order that they might obtain a place in heaven, and this was in spite of statements to the contrary in the scriptures. Tyndale wrote that, "If I live

---

1. William Tyndale, *Prelates, PS-2*, p. 337.
2. William Tyndale, *Answer, PS-3*, p. 161.

chaste, I do it not to obtain heaven thereby, for then should I do wrong to the blood of Christ: Christ's blood has obtained me that, Christ's merits have made me heir thereof."[1]

The pope claimed that he had power over the temporal as well as the spiritual realm. This applied not only to his power to control the government of countries but also to the rule of law so that the spiritualty could be protected when they had done wrong.

> The layman that had not done half so great faults must die, but the clerk must go escape free! Sent not the pope also unto the king of France remission of his sins, to go and conquer king John's realm? So now remission of sins cometh not by faith in the testament that God hath made in Christ's blood, but by fighting and murdering for the pope's pleasure.[2]

Tyndale also wrote that King Harold had exiled Robert, archbishop of Canterbury, and therefore, the pope gave a banner to William of Normandy to invade England. Therefore, we can see the ways by which the pope has strayed from Christ's pathway, when he sent William to fight against the Saxons:

> Here mark how straight the pope followeth Christ's steps and his apostles'! They preached forgiveness of sins to all that repented, through Christ's blood-shedding; the pope preacheth forgiveness of sins to all that will slay their brethren, bought with Christ's blood, to subdue them unto his tyranny.[3]

Tyndale listed many other ways by which the pope's Church led people away from the truth:

> And on the other side they had set up a righteousness of holy works to cleanse their souls withal; as the pope sanctifieth us with holy oil, holy bread, holy salt, holy candles, holy dumb ceremonies, and holy dumb blessings, and with whatsoever holiness thou wilt, save with the holiness of God's word; which only speaketh unto the heart, and sheweth the soul his filthiness and uncleanness of sin, and leadeth her by the way of repentance unto the fountain of Christ's blood, to wash it away through faith. By the reason of which false righteousness they were disobedient unto the righteousness of God, which is the forgiveness of sin in Christ's blood, and could not believe it.[4]

---

1. William Tyndale, *1525, New Testament*, p. 12.
2. William Tyndale, *Obedience, PS-1*, p. 339.
3. William Tyndale, *Prelates, PS-2*, p. 294.
4. William Tyndale, *Prologue Jonas, PS-1*, p. 462.

Tyndale expanded on these errors, and also on others that are not in that list, and we will be considering many of these in this chapter, as they affect Tyndale's understanding of the blood of Christ in scriptural theology against the teaching of the pope and his Church.

> They preach also, that the wagging of the bishop's hand over us blesseth us, and putteth away our sins. Are these works not against Christ? How can they do more shame unto Christ's blood? For if the wagging of the bishop's hand over me be so precious a thing in the sight of God that I am thereby blessed, how then am I full "blessed with all spiritual blessings in Christ?" as Paul saith, Eph. i.[1]

In his *A Dialogue Concerning Heresies*, Chapter 2 of Book 4, Thomas More attacks not only many of Luther's heresies but also Tyndale's. "And for a sample the author reherseth dyuers / wherof some be newe set forthe by Tyndall in hys englyshe bokys / wors yet in som parte than hys mayster Luther ys hym selfe." [2] One of the many errors that More found in Tyndale was, "Item he techeth that euery man & woman shold take ye holy sacrament / & spare not to touche yt & handell yt as mych as theym lyst."[3] Tyndale quoted part of More's charge and answered, "A perilous case. Why? Because the pope has not oiled them. Nevertheless, Christ hath anointed them with his Spirit and with his blood."[4] Tyndale continued that if the laity were allowed to handle the bread, they would realise that it was still bread and had not been transfigured into Christ's flesh. But according to the teaching of the pope's Church:

> Thou must believe that it is no more bread, but the very body of Christ, flesh, blood and bone, even as he went here on earth, save his coat: for that is here yet; I wot not in how many places. I pray thee, what helpeth all this? Here is no promise. The devils know that Christ died on a Friday, and the Jews also. What are they help thereby? We have a promise that Christ, and his body, and his blood, and all that he did and suffered, is a sacrifice, a ransom, and a full satisfaction for our sins; that God for his sake will think no more on them, if we have power to repent and believe.[5]

To ensure the smooth functioning of the Church, ceremonies and constitutions were introduced by apostles and early Christian leaders. These safeguarded the doctrine of Christ and were of value to everyone. But as

1. William Tyndale, *Obedience, PS-1*, p. 284.
2. Thomas More, *A Dialogue Concerning Heresies, CWM-6*, p. 348.
3. Ibid., p. 354.
4. William Tyndale, *Answer, PS-3*, p. 179.
5. William Tyndale, *Obedience, PS-1*, p. 278.

time passed and the needs of the Church changed, the spiritualty enhanced their power and moved away from the purity of the scriptures. Things had been altered:

> For by this time, what with the multitude of ceremonies, and heap of men's constitutions, whose right use was thereto clean forgotten, and partly because our shepherds were busied to seek themselves and their high authority, and exalted every man his throne, and were become wolves unto the flock, the cause why the people were disobedient unto wholesome counsel was, that the word of God was sore darkened, and no where purely preached. And therefore the prelates, loath to lose their high authority, and let the people go free of their yoke, began to turn their tale, and sing a new song, how that this penance was enjoined to make satisfaction to God for the sin that was committed; robbing our souls of the fruit of Christ's blood, and making us image-servants.[1]

Tyndale accused the Church of relying on the various ceremonies that the clergy had invented, or where they had imposed a new understanding for the meaning of these ceremonies and sacraments, often in order to enrich themselves and the Church.

> How many hundred thousand are there, which when they have sinned and knowledge their sins, yet trust in a bald ceremony, or in a lousy friars coat and merits; or in the prayers of them that devour widows' houses, and eat the poor out of house and harbour; in a thing of his own imagination; in a foolish dream, and a false vision; and not in Christ's blood, and in the truth that God hath sworn.[2]

The Church and Worship

Tyndale made a difference between those who went to church to worship God and those who thought that by going to church, by obediently following what they were told to do and by keeping the rules laid down by the church, they would go to heaven. Tyndale wrote about novices being professed as a friar,

> the father asketh him, Will you keep the rules of holy St. Francis? And he saith, Yea. . . . Then saith the father, And I promise you again everlasting life. O blasphemy! If eternal life be due unto the pilled traditions of lousy friars, where is the testament become that God made unto us in Christ's blood?"[3]

1. William Tyndale, *Exposiion 1 John, PS-2*, p. 161f.
2. William Tyndale, *Mammon, PS-1*, p. 122.
3. William Tyndale, *Obedience, PS-1*, p. 227.

Those the Church called heretics were those who, through their faith in Christ's blood, believed that it was shed for the forgiveness of their sins, who had found remission of sin and a new life as a child of God. Tyndale wrote of those condemned by the spiritualty, "That we now hate the devil's will (whereunto we were so fast locked, and could not but love it), is also the gift of Christ's blood; unto whom belongeth the praise and honour of our good deeds, and not unto us."[1]

Tyndale wrote that there are many different kinds of faiths that men have, but only one of them is of any value before God.

> The faith wherewith a man doth miracles is another gift than the faith of a repenting heart, to be saved through Christ's blood; and the one no kin to the other, though M. More would have them so appear. Neither is the devil's faith, and the pope's faith (wherewith they believe that there is a God, and that Christ is, and all the story of the bible, and may yet stand with all wickedness, and full consent to evil), kin unto the faith of them that hate evil, and repent of their misdeeds, and knowledge their sins, and be fled with full hope and trust of mercy unto the blood of Christ.[2]

The pope's Church leads people away from God, making them believe that the Christian is unable to approach God, but that he needs props and the help of saints if he is to expect God to help him grow in his Christian life. So, Tyndale wrote,

> Now let us come to the worshipping or honouring of sacraments, ceremonies, images, and relics. First, images be not God, and therefore no confidence is to be put in them. They are not made after the image of God, nor are the price of Christ's blood; but the workmanship of the craftsman, and the price of money, and therefore inferiors to man.[3]

Later on the same page Tyndale wrote about images and the ways in which man-made images caused people to waste their money, whilst neglecting to do their duty to care for people who had been made in the image of God.

> Images then, and relics, yea, and, as Christ saith, the holy day too, are servants unto man. And therefore it followeth, that we cannot, but unto our damnation, put on a coat worth an hundred coats upon a post's back, and let the image of God and the price of Christ's blood go up and down thereby naked. For if we care more to clothe the dead image

1. William Tyndale, *Pathway, PS-1*, p. 23.
2. William Tyndale, *Answer, PS-3*, p. 197.
3. Ibid., p. 59.

made by man, and the price of silver, than the lively image of God, and price of Christ's blood; then we dishonour the image of God, and him that made him, and the price of Christ's blood and him that bought him.[1]

Thomas More (*Dialogue, bk 2 ch. 11*) criticised the attack on the worship of images, claiming it was a different kind of worship to that which we gave to God. He also asked Tyndale if we should stop praying because "comenly in the wylde yrysshe and some in Wales to / as men say / whan they go forth in robbyng / they blysse them & pray god sende them good spede y[t] they may mete with a good purse & do harme & take none. Shall we therfore fynde a faute with euery mannes prayer bycause theues pray for spede in robbery?"[2] Tyndale's response to More was,

> And on the Sunday's God's word should be truly preached: which if his holy church would do, neither the Irish nor yet the Welsh would so pray; by which praying, and other like blindness, M. More may see that buzzing in Latin, on the holy days, helpeth not the hearts of the people. And I wonder that M. More can laugh at it, and not rather weep for compassion to see the souls for which Christ shed his blood to perish.[3]

The pope's Church also taught that the saints performed miracles, and these miracles showed that people believed

> he must be verily great with God! – and at once turn themselves from God's word, and put their trust and confidence in the saint and his merits; and make an advocate, or rather a god of the saint; and of their blind imagination make a testament, or bond, between the saint and them, the testament of Christ's blood clean forgotten.[4]

In this way, Tyndale believed that praying to saints was to turn man away from praying directly to God, but if it were God's will, God could send saints to help us: "And God hath bound himself, that if I come in the right way, by the door of Christ's blood, and ask help, that he will send me, if need be, an hundred legions of angels or saints.:" But we may not choose which saint God had to send. Tyndale then explained more clearly the errors of praying to saints:

> And yet we do worse than this: for we leave the way of Christ's blood, and go not to God through him; but run to the saints, in a testament of

---

1. Ibid.
2. Thomas More, *A Dialogue Concerning Heresies, CWM-6*, p. 236f.
3. William Tyndale, *Answer, PS-3*, p. 126.
4. William Tyndale, *Obedience, PS-1*, p. 184.

our own making, and will that they either save us themselves for our image-service, or compel God for their merit's sake to save us. Why goest thou not unto thy father thine ownself? 'I am a sinner,' will they say, 'and dare not.' If thou go in the right way, thou hast no sin. Christ hath taken all thy sins from thee; and God hath no rod in his hand, nor looketh sour, but merrily, that it is a lust to behold his cheerful countenance, and offereth thee his hand.[1]

Sacraments

Throughout his writings, Tyndale taught the significance of the sacraments of Baptism and the Lord's Supper; Baptism signified our new birth as a child of God and part of his family; the Lord's Supper signified being set free from our bondage to Satan, and the forgiveness of our sins through the blood of Christ. He also showed that all the papal sacraments had no significance because they claimed the power to fulfil God's purpose, even though they had no promise from God. Tyndale, therefore, criticised Thomas More's explanation of the sacraments:

> But when he leadeth me by the darkness of sacraments without signification, I cannot but catch harm, and put my trust and confidence in that which is neither God nor his word. As for an ensample, what trust put the people in anoiling, and how they cry for it, with no other knowledge than that the oil saveth them; unto their damnation, and denying of Christ's blood.[2]

Tyndale, in *The Practice of Prelates*, gave a potted history of the Church, and the way the spirituality became corrupted through claiming an importance for themselves, and acquiring lands and wealth, thereby straying from the teachings of Christ and his apostles. "Then, while they that had the plough by the tail looked back, the plough went awry; faith waxed feeble and fainty; love waxed cold; the scripture waxed dark; Christ was no more seen."[3] It was then that the Church lost the meaning of the ceremonies and sacraments.

> And as soon as the significance of the ceremonies was lost, and the priests preached Christ no longer, then the common people began to wax mad and out of their minds upon the ceremonies. And that trust and confidence which the ceremonies preached to be given unto God's word and Christ's blood, that same they turned unto the ceremony itself; as though a man were so mad to forget that the bush at the tavern-door did

1. William Tyndale, *Exposition 1 John, PS-2*, p. 167f.
2. William Tyndale, *Answer, PS-3*, p. 148f.
3. William Tyndale, *Prelates, PS-2*, p. 257.

signify wine to be sold within, but would believe that the bush itself would quench his thirst. And so they became servants unto the ceremonies; ascribing their justifying and salvation unto them, supposing that it was nothing else to be a christian man than to serve ceremonies, and him most christian that most served them; and contrariwise, him that was not popish and ceremonial, no christian man at all.[1]

The pope had become Christ's vicar, and he had the power to interpret the scriptures and to state what was truth and what was falsehood. Therefore, Christian doctrine was defined by the pope: "As when the pope saith, Ye be justified by the works of the ceremonies and sacraments, and so forth; and the scripture saith, that we be justified at the repentance of the heart, through Christ's blood."[2] Then, those who disagreed with the pope became heretics.

Tyndale wrote about the misuse of the Lord's Supper by those who did not receive it in the right spirit:

For, saith Paul, "Whosoever shall eat of this bread or drink of the cup of the Lord unworthily, shall be guilty of the body and blood of the Lord:" that is to say, whoso receiveth the sacrament of the body and blood of Christ with an unclean heart, not forsaking the old lusts of the flesh, nor purposing to follow Christ, and to be to his neighbour as Christ was to him, only merciful; the same sinneth against the body and blood of Christ; in that he maketh a mock of the earnest death of Christ, and, as it is written Hebrews the tenth, "treadeth Christ underfoot, and counteth the blood of the testament wherewith he was sanctified as an unholy thing, and doth dishonour to the Spirit of grace."[3]

Tyndale then went on to describe the three main ways by which Christ's words of institution were understood. Tyndale believed that transubstantiation and consubstantiation were wrong, and the true understanding was that "it is the memorial, the earnest, and seal of his body and blood, as the use of the scriptures is to call signs by the names of things signified thereby."[4]

The Roman Church had five other sacraments. Tyndale rejected these because they were without signification, and also had not been ordained by God. The most dangerous one was confession. Following Wyclif, who wrote, "Whether privy confession made to priests be needful to sinful men, and where this confession is grounded. And it seemeth that it is not needful, but brought in late by the fiend."[5] Tyndale said that confession was an

---

1. William Tyndale, *Answer, PS-3*, p. 76.
2. Ibid., p. 111.
3. William Tyndale, *Sacraments, PS-1*, p. 366.
4. Ibid., p. 371.
5. F.D. Matthew, *The English Works of Wyclif*, p. 328.

invention of Satan: "Shrift in the ear is verily a work of Satan; and that the falsest that ever was wrought, and that most hath devoured the faith."[1] This led on to many other errors in the pope's Church as the priest who heard one's confession gave the person a penance to perform.

> And the sacrament of penance they thus describe: contrition, confession, and satisfaction: contrition; sorrow for thy sins: confession; not to God and them whom thou hast offended, but tell thy sins in the priest's ear: satisfaction; to do certain deeds enjoined of them, to buy out thy sins. And in their description they have clean excluded the faith in the satisfaction of Christ's blood, which only bringeth life, and the spirit of life, and righteousness, and without the which it is impossible to please God: in whose stead they have put in the presumption of our own works. And for lack of trust in Christ's blood, our contrition is but a fruitless sorrow in the respect of hell, which maketh us hate the law still, and consequently God that made it.[2]

The spiritualty realised that, in spite of their claims to be able to forgive one's sins, it was only partly true. "For when they had put the satisfaction of Christ's blood out of the way, then as they compelled me to confess open sins, and to take open penance, even so they compelled them to confess secret sins, and to take secret penance."[3]

> And when God had promised the people a Saviour, to come and bless them, and save them from their sins; the Pharisees taught to believe in holy works to be saved by, as, if they offered and gave to be prayed for: as ours, as oft as we have a promise to be forgiven at the repentance of the heart through Christ's blood-shedding, put to, 'Thou must first shrive thyself to us of every syllable, and we must lay our hands on thine head, and whistle out thine sins, and enjoin thee penance to make satisfaction. And yet art thou but loosed from the sin only that thou shalt not come into hell; but thou must yet suffer for every sin seven years in purgatory, which is as hot as hell, except thou buy it out of the pope.'[4]

For purgatory was a money-making invention of the pope, and so Tyndale wrote, "shew the pope a little money, and God is so merciful that there is no purgatory. And why is not the fire out as well, if I offer for me the blood of Christ?"[5]

---

1. William Tyndale, *Obedience, PS-1*, p. 163.

2. William Tyndale, *Exposition 1 John, PS-2*, p. 162.

3. Ibid., p. 163.

4. William Tyndale, *Answer, PS-3*, p. 47.

5. Ibid., p. 143.

Thomas More, in his *Dialogue Concerning Heresy*, frequently felt that scripture and the church traditions were right in the understanding of Christian truths, rather than in Tyndale's interpretation of the word of God. Tyndale, in his *Answer*, would respond with, "I feel. . . . So, Tyndale wrote that More felt in his heart that there was a purgatory, but that he felt

> that every soul that beareth fruit in Christ, shall be purged of the Father to bear more fruit day by day, as it is written (John xv.), not in the pope's purgatory, where no man feeleth it, but here in this life such fruit as is unto his neighbour's profit; so that he which hath his hope in Christ purgeth himself here, as Christ is pure (1 John iii.); and that ever yet the blood of Jesus only doth purge us of all our sins, for the imperfectness of our works.[1]

Good Works

There were many ways by which the place of good works in the Christian's life was misunderstood by the Church before the Reformation. Tyndale wrote, "And so through their holy works done by the power of free will, they excluded themselves out of the holy rest of forgiveness of sins by faith in the blood of Christ."[2] The spirituality considered that these holy works were very important, for

> in these works they have so great confidence, that they not only trust to be saved thereby, and to be higher in heaven than they that be saved through Christ, but also promise to all other forgiveness of their sins through the merits of the same; wherein they rest, and teach other to rest also, excluding the whole world from the rest of forgiveness of sins through faith in Christ's blood.[3]

The spiritualty taught that it was possible for saints to do more good works than were necessary for their own salvation, and this surplus could be used by the pope to sell to those who have fallen short of earning their salvation by their own good works.

Although the monks spent a lot of time by fasting, thus earning more merits than they needed for their salvation, Tyndale questioned if there was any value in their fasting, even for their bodies, quite apart from their souls.

> The pope's fast is commonly only to eat no flesh. I say not, look how lean they be; but, consider what a taming of the flesh it is, to eat ten

---

1. Ibid., p. 142f.
2. William Tyndale, *Prologue Numbers, PS-1*, p. 429f.
3. Ibid., p. 431.

or twenty manner of fishes, dressed after the costliest manner, and to sit a couple of hours, and to pour in of the best wine and ale that may be gotten; and at night to banquet of dew (as they say) of all manner of fruits and confections, marmalade, succade, green ginger, comfits sugarplate with malmsey and romney burnt with sugar, cinnamon and cloves, with bastado, muscadell and ipocrass, &c. Think ye not that a piece of salt fish or pickeral, with drinking and such dews, doth not tame the body exceedingly?[1]

And so, Tyndale wrote of the way merits were obtained by monks through their prayers and fasting, and he gave 'proofs' why these works of supererogation failed.

Another proof is that they so long a time have given pardons, of the merits of their fasting, as though they had done more than enough for themselves; and of that merchandise have gotten all they have, and have brought the knowledge of Christ's blood clean into darkness.[2]

For God does not delight in our pain-taking and our fasting, but in our true obedience to his commandment to love our neighbour. "If thou do it of vain-glory, to have the praise that belongeth to God, or for a greater profit only, or to make satisfaction for thy sins past, and to dishonour Christ's blood, which hath made it already; then is thine alms abominable."[3]

In *The Prologue to the Book of Numbers*, Tyndale wrote that God had ended the animal sacrifices for the forgiveness of sins, Hebrews 10. It is only the sacrificial blood of Christ that is sufficient for all we need; the sacrifices that the papal church makes are of no value at all for man's salvation.

For in him God hath promised not forgiveness of sins only, but also whatsoever we ask to keep us from sin and temptation withal. And what if thou burn frankincense unto him, what if thou a candle, what if thou burn thy chastity or virginity unto him for the same purpose, dost thou not like rebuke unto Christ's blood? Moreover, if thou offer gold, silver, or any other good for the same intent, is there any difference? And even so, if thou go on pilgrimage, or fastest, or goest woolward, or sprinklest thyself with holy water, or whatsoever deed it is, or observest whatsoever ceremony it be, for like meaning, then it is like abomination.[4]

---

1. William Tyndale, *Exposition Matthew, PS-2*, p. 97.
2. Ibid., p. 98.
3. Ibid., p. 96.
4. William Tyndale, *Prologue Numbers, PS-1*, p. 433.

The spiritualty have, by their false doctrines, led the Christian church astray from the truths that God has given us in the scriptures and substituted these truths with their man made ideas, even as Satan had led Adam and Eve astray and brought sin and death into the world. Tyndale asked:

> For unto what further blindness could all the devils in hell bring them, than to make them believe that they were justified through their own good works? For when they once believed that they were purged from their sins, and made righteous through their own holy works, what room was there left for the righteousness that is in Christ's blood-shedding?[1]

The result is that the papal Christian cannot see the truth of the gospel nor the right way that leads to our justification, and we stumble on our life's journey.

> How dark is the doctrine of them that teach that a man may compel God, with the works of free-will, to give him his favour and grace; or make God unrighteous! How dark is the doctrine of them which (to the rebuke of Christ's blood) teach that works do justify before God, and make satisfaction for sins![2]

Those who did not agree with the doctrines of the spiritualty but believed in the truth of God's word were called heretics by the papists. Tyndale argued against More's claim that images in churches should be kept and that the worship offered to them was different from the worship of God. More wrote, "Neyther the bysshoppe of Massyle that brake the ymagis that they speke of / nor the counsayle of grece neyther scismatycall as it was / went neuer yet so farr as Luther and Tyndall and theyr company do / whych not onely set at nought ymagis but also leue no saynt vnblasphemed / nor Cristes own mother neyther."[3] Tyndale replied to More: "Now answer me, by what reason canst thou make an heretic of him that concludeth nought against God, but worketh with God, and putteth that block [image] out of the way, whereat his brother, the price of Christ's blood, stumbleth and loseth his soul?"[4]

William Tracy had been condemned as a heretic because in his will he had left no money for any prayers for his soul

> when most need is to be strong, and fear the pope's purgatory, and trust to the prayer of priests dearly paid for? I dare say that he prayed for the

---

1. Ibid., p. 432.
2. William Tyndale, *Exposition Matthew, PS-2*, p. 103.
3. Thomas More, *A Dialogue Concerning Heresies, CWM-6*, p. 359.
4. William Tyndale, *Answer, PS-3*, p. 183.

priests when he died, that God would convert a great many of them; and if he had known of any good man among them that had needed, he would have given; and if he had known of any lack of priests, he would have given to maintain more. But now, since there be more than enough, and have more than every man a sufficient living, how should he have given them, to hire their prayers, but of pure mistrust in Christ's blood?[1]

Summary

We have seen many ways by which the spiritualty had turned from God's word and substituted it with their own ideas, showing how they were able, by their good works and beliefs, to do what was pleasing to God. Tyndale commented frequently on their errors, showing that they had rejected God's way of salvation through the blood of Christ and substituted their own efforts for God to accept for their justification. He also condemned the false ideas that the papal Church had introduced which, in the Mass, gave power to the priest to enable him to change the bread into Christ's body and the wine into Christ's blood. Many of the other false teachings had led to the enrichment of the church, through confession, purgatory and the sale of indulgences.

> Whosoever goeth about to make satisfaction for his sins to God-ward, saying in his heart, This much have I sinned, this much will I do again; or this-wise will I live to make amends withal, or this will I do, to get to heaven withal, the same is an infidel, faithless, and damned in his deed-doing, and hath lost his part in Christ's blood; because he is disobedient unto God's testament, and setteth up another of his own imagination, unto which he will compel God to obey.[2]

Tyndale, in his *Exposition of Matthew*, commenting on the statement, "If therefore the light that is in thee be darkness, how great is that darkness!" criticised the papist, in the following terms:

> How dark is the doctrine of them which (to the rebuke of Christ's blood) teach that works do justify before God, and make satisfaction for sins! How blind are they that think prayer to be the pattering of many words; and will therefore not only be praised and paid of the world, but also by the title thereof challenge heaven, and not by the merits of Christ's blood.[3]

---

1. William Tyndale, *Exposition Tracy's Will, PS-3*, p. 279f.
2. William Tyndale, *Obedience, PS-1*, p. 228.
3. William Tyndale, *Exposition Matthew, PS-2*, p. 103.

Tyndale mentioned the darkness that overwhelmed the papal Church, covering many other doctrines where they erred.

This had led the papist church to attack those whose faith was in Christ's blood for their salvation, calling them 'heretics' and 'unbelievers', arresting them, punishing them and sending many of them to be burnt at the stake. However, this enmity was not a surprise to those who trusted in God.

> Christ warned his disciples at his last supper, to have peace in him; affirming that they should have none in the world. The false prophets shall ever impugn the faith in Christ's blood, and enforce to quench the true understanding of the law, and the right meaning and intent of all the works commanded by God; which fight is a fight above all fights.[1]

In his *Supplication to the King*, Tyndale called on Christians not to be led astray by the spiritualty:

> But if it be of a set malice against the truth, and of a grounded hate against the law of God, by a reason of a full consent they have to sin, and to walk in their old ways of ignorance, whereunto, being now past all repentance, they have utterly yielded themselves, to follow with full lust, without bridle or snaffle (which is the sin against the Holy Ghost), then ye shall see, even shortly, that God shall turn the point of the sword wherewith they now shed Christ's blood, homeward, to shed their own again, after all the examples of the Bible.[2]

Tyndale did not recognise that there was anything good in the Church of Rome. Unlike Luther and some other Reformers, he could never have agreed that:

> Although the city of Rome is worse than Sodom and Gomorra, nevertheless there remain in it Baptism, the Sacrament, the voice and text of the Gospel, the Sacred Scriptures, the ministries, the name of Christ, and the name of God. Whoever has these, has them; whoever does not have them, has no excuse, for the treasure is still there. Therefore the Church of Rome is holy, because it has the holy name of God, the Gospel, Baptism, etc. If these are present among a people, that people is called holy."[3]

For Tyndale, although the Church of Rome had the names of the signs of the Church, unlike Luther, Tyndale rejected their teaching of those signs, and wrote,

---

1. Ibid., p. 116.
2. William Tyndale, *Supplication to the King, A & M, vol 5*, p. 131.
3. Martin Luther, *Lectures on Galatians, 1535, LW-26*, p. 24.

They have robbed Christ of all his merits, and clothed themselves therewith. They have robbed the soul of man of the bread of her life, the faith and trust in Christ's blood; and have fed her with the shales and cods of the hope in their merits and confidence in their good works.[1]

For it was not just a few errors that were found in the Church of Rome, but

a thousand such superstitiousnesses setteth he before us, instead of Christ to believe in; neither Christ nor God's word, neither honourable to God nor serviceable unto our neighbour, nor profitable unto ourselves for the taming of the flesh; which all are the denying of Christ's blood.[2]

---

1. William Tyndale, *Exposition Matthew, PS-2*, p. 122f.
2. William Tyndale, *Answer, PS-3*, p. 40.

7. Conclusion

Sola Scriptura

William Tyndale believed that *sola scriptura* meant the whole Bible, from Genesis 1 to Revelation 22, is a single book and that there is a continuity throughout the Bible. Unlike many Christians, he did not believe that there was a break between the Old Testament and the New, and that the time of Christ heralded a new beginning to God's plan for man's reconciliation to God.

Beginning with Paul's statement regarding Christ in Ephesians 1:4 that God "chose us in him before the foundation of the world," Tyndale made the starting point for man's salvation before God created the world. Therefore, the scriptures point us to God's plan for the restoration of creation to its pristine state before Adam's disobedience to God's command had destroyed the goodness of the world's creation. Although Tyndale's concern is with the restoration of man, rather than with the restoration of creation, it is easy to see that there is a link between the two.

Following the Fall and Adam's disobedience to God's command, God's plan for the restoration of man started to unfold. God had given charge to Adam to look after and to care for the world he had created; everything was provided for Adam's needs, and for those of his wife, Eve. However, there was one thing forbidden, he must not eat of the tree of knowledge; if he did, he would die. But Satan wanted to deprive God of his creation and to usurp Adam's rule over the earth. So, Satan tempted Adam and Eve, saying that they would not die even if they ate the tree of knowledge. They believed Satan, ate of the tree, and they died spiritually. God cast them out of the Garden of Eden and prevented their return. But before that, he gave Adam and Eve a glimmer of hope. One day, a man would be born who would destroy the power of Satan and restore man to his pre-Fall condition.

Sola Scriptura created some problems. There were some who thought that the scriptures raised some questions in their minds but did not provide a clear answer to them; but they needed to see how these questions might be resolved. Tyndale rejected every speculation where Christians tried to find an answer when the word of God left some things unexplained. The most important unanswered question concerned God's predestination and who God had chosen to save. Tyndale believed that it was a question we should not try to answer.

> But here must a mark be set to those unquiet, busy, and high-climbing spirits, how far they shall go; which first of all bring hither their high reasons and pregnant wits, and begin first from an high to search the bottomless secrets of God's predestination, whether they be predestinate or not.[1]

In that way, against some Reformers, Tyndale's *sola scriptura* will not allow him to speculate on God's "bottomless secrets", especially on who is predestinated to eternal life and who is not. Tyndale's theology only looks at God's election to eternal life. In fact, because natural man is already dead in sin, Tyndale has no place for some being predestined to eternal death (double predestination).

It is through Tyndale's belief that we have to rely on the scriptures for our doctrine; that he was brought to realise the importance of Christ's blood in God's plan to restore man and creation to its original goodness. The blood of Christ cannot be ignored as we seek to make sense of God's revelation in the Bible. For Christ's sacrifice and blood-shedding is the only way by which man can be forgiven for his disobedience to God's commands and enabled to be born again to live faithfully as a child of God.

Many of Tyndale's attacks on the papist Church come from their deviations from the literal sense of scripture. Tyndale complains of the many different interpretations and doctrines that the scholastic doctors make, and he makes a list of some of those doctors, before continuing, "and such like out of number;" in fact, Tyndale says that the largest warehouse would not be big enough to house one book from each doctor who taught a different interpretation of scripture. "In so great diversity of spirits, how shall I know who lieth, and who sayeth truth? Whereby shall I try and judge them? Verily by God's word, which only is true. But how shall I that do, when thou wilt not let me see scripture?"[2]

Tyndale taught that the only important way for us to know God's will and how to be a Christian and live a Christian life was through the scriptures.

> Christ commandeth to search the scriptures. John v. Though that miracles bare record unto his doctrine, yet desired he no faith to be given either to his doctrine, or to his miracles, without record of the scriptures. When Paul preached, Acts xvii. the other searched the scriptures daily, whether

---

1. William Tyndale, *Prologue Romans, PS-1*, p. 505f.
2. William Tyndale, *Obedience, PS-1*, p. 153.

they were as he alleged them. Why shall I not likewise see, whether it be the scripture that thou allegest? Yea, why shall I not see the scripture, and the circumstances, and what goeth before and after; that I may know whether thine interpretation be the right sense, or whether thou jugglest, and drawest the scripture violently unto thy carnal and fleshly purpose; or whether thou be about to teach me, or to deceive me.[1]

The Blood of Christ

The hardest decision that anyone has to make while attempting to cover the full implication of the theology of Christ's blood in Tyndale's theology is what should be included and what should be left out. I started with 342 extracts from Tyndale's writings, many of them applying to several doctrines. Tyndale's theology of Christ's blood covers every doctrine relating to man and his life as a child of God. It also shows man's errors, whether they occurred through a false interpretation of scripture or through the traditions of the sixteenth-century Roman Catholic Church or through unbelief. I hope that for the the doctrines that I have not included and for the extracts that I have chosen to omit, Tyndale does not look over my shoulder and say "Why didn't you include that?" This is especially true where I have not included some quotations in my study of '*The Blood of Christ*'.[2]

I was very conscious that in writing about one doctrine only, there are many questions that almost demand answering, often when it seems to introduce other doctrines. I can almost hear you saying, 'That seems to demand expounding.' This is especially true when, for Tyndale, it is the blood of Christ, because every doctrine related to our becoming Christians, and our Christian life depends for its validity on Christ's blood.

When I started my research into Tyndale's theology, I soon realised that I would have to make a lot of revisions to every theological position I had ever come across. Whatever theology I had studied had meant that I was left with some unanswered theological questions. Before Tyndale, I had considered that Calvin was the most scriptural of all Reformation theologians. Yet, I found that his theology left me with a number of questions where I could not find scriptural answers. I also found some 'answers' that I could not justify from my reading of the Bible, especially some statements about predestination.

Tyndale was different. He brought a completely new vision to biblical theology. Every doctrine had to be compatible with every other doctrine, and with the scriptures of the Old and New Testaments. However, he acknowledged that we would find some questions to which God had not provided answers, and said that we should not try to find one where God had not revealed his secret will.

---

1. Ibid., p. 146f.
2. See Appendix 2 for all references to Christ's blood.

God's plan for man's salvation started before creation, for he knew that Satan would not rest until he had destroyed the beauty and goodness of the world that God was going to create. God also knew that the Devil would deceive man and cause him to sin. Therefore, the Persons of the Trinity made a covenant between themselves on how Satan's power could be destroyed and how the harm he had done to man and the world could be set right and the world restored to its pristine goodness.

Genesis begins with God's creation of the world and of his giving man the command to rule and care for God's world. Satan deceived man, and, as a result, man became Satan's slave. Man's punishment was to die spiritually, and God drove Adam and Eve out of the Garden of Eden. However, God's plan to destroy Satan and to restore the world and man to their primal state began, even as man was driven out and barred from returning to the Garden of Eden. Tyndale believed that the Scriptures teach us that we cannot make a division between the Old and the New Testaments – for they form God's continuous plan for man's salvation through Christ's sacrifice on the Cross. Man's salvation began with the blood of animal sacrifices that pointed to Christ's sacrificial blood, which one day was to be shed for us, but it did not make a new start when Jesus died upon the Cross. When Christ, the Lamb of God, shed his blood, the final sacrifice had been made, and the sacrifices in the Old Testament had fulfilled their function and were no longer of value.

Over the course of time, from the Fall to Christ's ministry, we find God's plan for salvation being unfolded. God used 'pictures' or 'signs' to teach his people, so that they could begin to understand God's plan that enabled them to be his people.

> After that he made a covenant with Abraham, to be his God, and the God of his posterity, and their shield and defender; and Abraham promised for him and his seed to be his people, and to believe and trust in him, and to keep his commandments; which covenant God caused to be written in the flesh of Abraham and the males of his posterity, commanding the males to be circumcised the eighth day, or to be slain: which circumcision was the seal and obligation of the said covenant.[1]

In circumcision, the child's blood was shed, a sign that he had become a member of God's covenant with man. After Christ had shed his blood, the covenant sign, circumcision, which was accompanied by blood being shed, was replaced by water representing Christ's blood; circumcision was replaced by baptism.

The next picture was when God told Abraham to sacrifice his son Isaac. At the last moment, God stopped Abraham, and Isaac's blood was replaced by the blood of the ram that had been caught in a thicket.

---

1. William Tyndale, *Sacraments, PS-1*, p. 349.

Tyndale makes us realise that man is a slave of Satan. He used the sign of the Israelites being slaves to Pharaoh in Egypt and that they had to obey the one who owned them. Eventually, God ensured that the Israelites would be freed from the pharaoh's bondage. Following the plagues that God sent to inflict the Egyptians, God gave the Israelites the Passover lamb to be a sacrifice, whose blood, on the door-posts of the Israelite houses, was to set the Israelites free from their slavery. This pictured Christ, our Passover lamb, who was sacrificed for us (1 Cor. 5:7).

The Children of Israel then set out on their journey to the Promised Land, and the blood of their sacrifices, sprinkled on them by the priest, was to keep them faithful as God's children during their wanderings. Tyndale believed that this illustrated our Christian life, from the day we were set free from Satan's bondage until we, at last, enter our Promised Land where we will be eternally in God's presence. The Holy Spirit sprinkles the blood of Christ on the Christian during his journey for "the blood of Jesus his Son cleanseth us from all sin" (1 Jn 1:7). Tyndale taught that the blood in the Old Testament sacrifices represented the blood of Christ that one day was going to be shed. God accepted their sacrifices, but after Christ had died, and his blood shed, the animal sacrifices ceased, because the blood they represented had at last been shed.

As we have seen, the two major 'sacraments' of the Old Testament; circumcision and the Passover, in both of which blood was shed, were replaced by the bloodless sacrifices of the Christian Church, baptism, "And instead of circumcision came our baptism."[1] The Lord's Supper was the fulfilment of the Passover, for, as Tyndale wrote,

> Neither was it the lamb's blood that delivered you then: . . . but the blood of Christ (whom that lamb figured, and described his innocence, pureness, and obedience to his Father, and compassion to mankind-ward, whose feeble nature he had put on with all the infirmities of the same, save sin) did then deliver you.[2]

We followed through the Christian's life, the importance of Christ's blood at every stage of our journey to our Promised Land and the way the Old Testament helps us to understand the outworking of our Christian faith. God gave the Children of Israel his laws, and summarised them in Leviticus and Deuteronomy, and in the Gospels we find Jesus stressing the importance of this summary. Jesus asked the lawyer "What is written in the law?" The lawyer quoted those two verses. (Lk. 10:26.), and Jesus quoted them, Matthew 22:37-39. "Thou shalt love the Lord thy God with all thy

---

1. William Tyndale, *Sacraments, PS-1*, p. 350f.
2. Ibid., p. 355.

heart, and with all thy soul, and with all thy mind. . . . Thou shalt love thy neighbour as thyself." Tyndale stressed the importance of those two laws for the Christian's life as a child of God throughout his writings.

Summary

The importance of the blood of Christ begins with God and continues throughout God's plans to restore man, and also fallen creation, to their pristine purity. God made his covenant which was to destroy Satan and restore man and God's creation to the purity they possessed before man succumbed to Satan's temptation. And so, through Christ's sacrifice of himself upon the Cross, man was able to be at peace with God. In describing this, Tyndale could not refrain from making a snide remark about the pope's false claims.

> For the conditions of the peace that is made between God and us in Christ's blood are these: The law is set before us, unto which if we consent and submit ourselves to be scholars thereof, then are not only all our fore sins forgiven, both *pœna et culpa* (with our holy father's licence ever); but also all our infirmities, weakness, proneness, readiness, and motions unto sin, are pardoned and taken aworth, and we translated from under the damnation of the law, which damneth as well those infirmities as the sin that springeth of them, and putteth us under grace, (Rom. vii.): so that we shall not henceforth, as long as we forsake not our profession, be judged by the rigorousness of the law; but chastised, if we do amiss, as children that are under no law.[1]

The whole of man's salvation, the power for him to live as a child of God, and for him to care for and look after God's world, depends on the blood of Christ. Through the Holy Spirit's work, the blood of Christ cleanses and empowers the Christian to do God's will. Tyndale saw what this entailed for the person re-created by the blood of Christ, and how this blood enabled him to love and serve God, to love his neighbour as himself and to do his Father's will by his good works, until he entered God's eternal kingdom of heaven.

The Papal Church

It is through Tyndale's theology that we find that most often his criticism of the Roman Church lies in its interpretation of the scriptures, although there are many instances where he attacks scholasticism and its reliance on Aristotle. *The Practice of Prelates* is largely an attack on the pope's attitude to scripture, where he teaches his own interpretation in order to enhance his own authority and increase the power and wealth of the Church. There is

1. William Tyndale, *Exposition 1 John, PS-2*, p. 155-60.

also Tyndale's attack on the pope's Church in *The Obedience of a Christian Man*, where Tyndale exposes the errors of scholasticism. "Is it not a madness then to say, that we could not understand the scripture without Aristotle?" The student goes to University where they

> drive them from God's word, and will let no man come thereto, until he have been two years master of art. First they nosel them into sophistry, and in *benefundatum*. and there corrupt their judgements with apparent arguments, and with alleging unto them texts of logic, of natural *philautia*, of metaphysic, and moral philosophy, and of all manner of books of Aristotle. . . . When they have likewise brawled eight, ten, or twelve or more years, and after that their judgements are utterly corrupt, then they begin their divinity; not at the scripture, but every man taketh a sundry doctor.

Tyndale then lists the various ways in which the student is confused and driven from an understanding of the scriptures; finally stating, "God is not man's imagination; but that only which he saith of himself. . . . God is but his word, as Christ saith, John viii. 'I am that I say unto you;' that is to say, That which I preach am I; my words are spirit and life."[1]

I leave the final word to Tyndale:

> So now thou seest that life eternal and all good things are promised unto faith and belief; so that he that believeth on Christ shall be safe. Christ's blood hath purchased life for us, and made us the heirs of God; so that heaven cometh by Christ's blood. If thou wouldest obtain heaven with the merits and deservings of thine own works, so didst thou wrong, yea, and shamedst, the blood of Christ; and unto thee were Christ dead in vain. Now is the true believer the heir of God by Christ's deservings; yea, and in Christ was predestinate, and ordained unto eternal life, before the world began. . . . So let thine eye be single, and look unto good living only, and take no thought for the reward, but be content: forasmuch as thou knowest and art sure, that the reward, and all things contained in God's promises, follow good living naturally; and thy good works do but testify only, and certify thee that the Spirit of God is in thee, whom thou hast received as an earnest of God's truth; and that thou art heir of all the goodness of God, and that all good things are thine already, purchased by Christ's blood, and laid up in store against that day, when every man shall receive according to his deeds, that is, according as his deeds declare and testify what he is or was.[2]

---

1. William Tyndale, *Obedience, PS-1*, pp. 156–60.
2. William Tyndale, *Mammon, PS-1*, p. 65f.

Appendix 1:

Numbers of Occurrences of "blood of Christ" in Tyndale's Writings

Except *1525 New Testament, 1534 New Testament* and *Tyndale's Supplication to the King*, the remainder are from The Parker Society Edition of Tyndale's Works and Foxe, *The Acts and Monuments*, vol 5 pt. 1..

(The first number: number of times 'blood' occurs in the work. The second number: total number of words divided by occurrences of 'blood of Christ'.)

1525 New Testament
23   575 words/blood of Christ. (This figure would be greatly reduced if the 'marginal notes' were omitted and only the 'Preface' used: this reduces to 493 words/blood of Christ.)

A Pathway into the Holy Scripture

26   331 words/blood of Christ

The Parable of the Wicked Mammon

44   747 words/blood of Christ

The Obedience of a Christian Man

34   2570 words/blood of Christ

A Brief Declaration of the Sacraments

38   525 words/blood of Christ

Tyndale's Epistle to the Reader, 1526 New Testament

4   382 words/blood of Christ

Prologue to the Book of Genesis

2   844 words/blood of Christ

Prologue to Exodus

1   3174 words/blood of Christ

Prologue to Leviticus

10   473 words/blood of Christ

Prologue to Numbers

9   526 words/blood of Christ

Prologue to Deuteronomy

1   1602 words/blood of Christ

Prologue to the Prophet Jonas

10   732 words/blood of Christ

Prologue upon the Gospel of St Matthew

8   158 words/blood of Christ

Prologue upon the Epistle of St Paul to the Romans

3   3636 words/blood of Christ

Prologue upon the Epistle of Paul to Titus

1   215 words/blood of Christ

Prologue upon the Epistle of Paul to the Hebrews

2   1493 words/blood of Christ

Prologue upon the Epistle of St James

1   523 words/blood of Christ

Prologue upon the First Epistle of Peter

1   412 words/blood of Christ

Prologue upon the Three Epistles of St John

1   392 words/blood of Christ

Exposition upon the Fifth, Sixth and Seventh Chapters of Matthew

40   1374 words/blood of Christ

Exposition of the First Epistle of Saint John

59   660 words/blood of Christ

The Practice of Prelates

10   3673 words/blood of Christ

Answer to Sir Thomas More's Dialogue

78   1125 words/blood of Christ

Exposition of the Testament of Master William Tracy

13   455 words/blood of Christ

Tyndale's Supplication to the King, Nobles and Subjects of England A & M, vol. 5, pt 1, pp. 130–1

2   381 words/blood of Christ

Tyndale refers to the blood of Christ on 441 occasions in a theological way, covering every aspect of his theology, compared with his only mentioning the cross of Christ, relating to Christ's death on the cross for our salvation, in a theological way three times, *Prologue Exodus*, PS-1, p. 412: *Prologue Leviticus*, PS-1, p. 124 and in *Answer*, PS-3, p. 149, Tyndale linked both cross and blood, when he answered More's statement, 'The priest offereth, or sacrificeth Christ's body'; twice he said that, in the Mass, the priest did not break Christ's body nor shed his blood; he then explained the true meaning of the Lord's Supper thus:

> Let no man beguile you with his juggling sophistry. Our offering of Christ is to believe in him, and to come with a repenting heart unto the remembrance of his passion; and to desire God the Father, for the breaking of Christ's body on the cross, and shedding of his blood, and for his death, and all his passions, to be merciful unto us, and to forgive us, according to his testament and promise: and so we receive forgiveness of our sins. And other offering or sacrificing of Christ, is there now none.[1]

From this list, we can see that 'the blood of Christ' is fairly evenly divided in each of Tyndale's writings, and, as we would expect from the subject matter, it appears less frequently (for the number of words) in *The Practice of Prelates*. Perhaps the surprise lies in the fact that for the number of words in the *1525 New Testament*, the 'blood of Christ' appears more than we would expect. Otherwise, the variation in the density of the phrase for the length of the writing is not so great.

---

1. William Tyndale, *Answer, PS-3*, p. 149.

Appendix 2:

Complete References to "blood of Christ" in Tyndale's Writings

Authorial Note

These extracts from Tyndale's writings are mainly taken from the Parker Society edition of his Works, and generally are taken from his text, but not his 'marginal notes', unless the marginal note contain material not in the text. I have also changed 'father' into 'Father' where it refers to God, and also one or two other words where capital letters 'modernised' Tyndale's spelling. The extracts from the *1525, New Testament* (Edward Arber, Facsimile, 1871) also include Tyndale's marginal notes; and the *1526 Prologue to the Romans* (EEBO), extracts have their spelling and punctuation modernised.

Some of the quotations from Tyndale's writings are quite short and can stand on their own, other quotations have the context from Tyndale's work so that they can be understood; however, they all benefit when looked at within Tyndale's writing.

Apart from the *1525, New Testament* and *1526 Prologue to Romans*, the order of the rest of Tyndale's writings are roughly in date order, rather than their position in the Parker Society volumes. *The Supper of the Lord* has not been included as it is considered to be a work of George Joye. I believe the evidence for Joye's authorship is very strong, and also that the theology of *The Supper* is different to Tyndale's.

Where there is any ambiguity about the matter quoted, whether as text or marginal note, the abbreviations 'Txt.' and 'Mg.' have been used to distinguish them.

1525, New Testament (Arber)

1. 4. In the gospel when we believe the promises, we receive the Spirit of life, and are justified in the blood of Christ from all things whereof the law condemned us.

2. 5. I must also have the promises before my eyes that I despair not, in which promises I see the mercy, favour, and good will of God upon me in the blood of his Son Christ; who has made satisfaction for my unperfectness, and fulfilled for me, that which I could not do.

3.   7f. In Christ God loved us his elect and chosen before the world began, and reserved us unto the knowledge of his Son and of his holy gospel, and when the gospel is preached he openeth our hearts, and giveth us grace to believe, and putteth the Spirit of Christ in us; and we know him as our Father most merciful; and consent to the law, and love it inwardly in our heart; and desire to fulfil it, and sorrow because we cannot, which will (sin we of frailty never so much) is sufficient till more strength be given us, the blood of Christ has made satisfaction for the rest: the blood of Christ has obtained all things for us of God. Christ is our satisfaction, redeemer, deliverer, saviour from vengeance and wrath. Observe and mark in the pistles of Paul, and Peter, and in the gospel and pistles of John what Christ is unto us.

4.   8. The cause is verily, that except a man cast away his own imagination and reason he cannot perceive God, and understand the virtue and power of the blood of Christ.

5.   9. The Evangelion shows unto him the promises of God in Christ; and how that Christ has purchased pardon for him, has satisfied the law for him, and peaced the wrath of God; and the poor sinner believes, lauds and thanks God through Christ, and breaks out into exceeding inward joy and gladness, for that he has escaped so great wrath, so heavy vengeance, so fearful and so everlasting a death: and he henceforth is hungry and thirsty after more righteousness, that he might fulfil the law; and mourns continually commending his weakness unto God in the blood of our Saviour Jesus Christ.

6.   10. It is not possible for a natural man to consent to the law that it should be good, or that God should be righteous who made the law. Man's wit, reason, and will, are so fast glued, yea, nailed and chained unto the will of the devil. Neither can any creature loose the bonds, save the blood of Christ.

7.   10. This is the captivity and bondage whence Christ delivered us, redeemed, and loosed us. His blood, his death, his patience, in suffering rebukes and wrongs, his prayers and fastings, his meekness and fulfilling of the utmost point of the law, peaced the wrath of God, brought the favour of God to us again; obtained that God should love us first, and be our Father, and that a merciful Father; that will consider our infirmities and weakness, and will give us his Spirit again (which was taken away in the fall of Adam) to rule, govern, and strength us, and to break the bonds of Satan, wherein we were so strait bound.

8.   11. Now Christ stands us in double stead, and serves us two manner wise. First he is our redeemer, deliverer, reconciler, mediator, intercessor, advocate, attorney, solicitor, our hope, comfort, shield, protection, defender, strength, health, satisfaction, and salvation. His blood, his death,

all that he ever did is ours. And Christ himself, with all that he is or can do, is ours. His blood shedding and all that he did, does me as good service as though I myself had done it.

9.　11. Whatsoever therefore faith has received of God through Christ's blood and deserving, that same must love shed out everywhit, and bestow it on our neighbours unto their profit; yea, and that though they be our enemies.

10.　12. If I live chaste, I do it not to obtain heaven thereby. For then should I do wrong to the blood of Christ: Christ's blood has obtained me that, Christ's merits have made me heir thereof.

11.　13. Who shall separate us from the love that God loves us withal: that is to say, what shall make me believe God loves me not: Shall tribulation, Anguish, Persecution, Shall hunger, Nakedness, Shall a sword: Nay, I am sure that neither death, nor life, neither angel, neither rule, nor power, neither present things, nor things to come, neither high nor low, neither any creature is able to separate us from the love of God which is in Christ Jesu our Lord. In all such tribulations a Christian man perceives that God is his Father, and loves him, even as he loved Christ when he shed his blood on the cross.

12.　14. Even so now since I am coupled to God by Christ's blood, do I well; not for heaven's sake, but because I am heir of heaven by grace and Christ's purchasing; and have the Spirit of God. I do good freely, for so is my nature. As a good tree brings forth good fruit: and an evil tree, evil fruit.

13.　14. Whatsoever is our own is sin. Whatsoever is above that is Christ's gift, purchase, doing and working. He bought us of his Father dearly with his blood; yea, with his most bitter death and gave his life for it. Whatsoever good thing is in us, that is given us freely without our deserving or merits for Christ's blood's sake. That we desire to follow the will of God, it is the gift of Christ's blood. That we now hate the devil's will (whereunto we were so fast locked, and could not but love it) is also the gift of Christ's blood; unto whom belongeth the praise and honour of our good deeds, and not unto us.

14.　23. Mg Mt. 5. Beatitudes. For all good things are given to us freely of God for Christ's blood's sake and his merits.

15.　27. Mg Mt, 6. For all good things come of the bountifulness, liberality, mercy, promises, and truth of God by the deserving of Christ's blood only.

16.　27. Mg Mt. 6. Single. The eye is single when a man in all his deeds looks but on the will of God, and looks not for laud, honour, or any other reward in this world; neither ascribes heaven or a higher room in heaven unto his deeds. But accepts heaven as a thing purchased by the blood of Christ, and works freely for love's sake only.

17.　61. Mg Mt. 21. 'John came in way of righteousness.' John taught the very way unto righteousness, for he interpreted the law right, and damned man and all his deeds and righteousness, and drove men unto Christ, to seek true righteousness through mercy obtained in his blood.

Prologue to the Epistle To Romans, 1526 (EEBO)

1. a iiii. Now is the Spirit no otherwise given than by faith only, in that we believe the promises of God, without wavering, how that God is true, and will fulfil all his good promises to usward, for the blood of Christ's sake, as it is plain in the first chapter.

2. b ij. Abraham's circumcision was an outward sign, whereby he declared his righteousness, which he had by faith, and his obedience and readiness unto the will of God; even so are all the other good works outward signs and outward fruits of faith and of the Spirit: which do not justify a man, but that a man is justified already before God inwardly in the heart, through faith and through the Spirit purchased by Christ's blood.

3. b vi. Wherefore of a man's own strength is the law never fulfilled, we must have thereunto God's favour and his Spirit, purchased by Christ's blood.

Mammon – Blood of Christ (PS-1)

1. 48. If thou wilt therefore be at peace with God, and love him, thou must turn to the promises of God, and to the gospel, which is called of Paul, in the place before rehearsed to the Corinthians, the ministration of righteousness, and of the Spirit. For faith bringeth pardon and forgiveness freely purchased by Christ's blood, and bringeth also the Spirit; the Spirit looseth the bonds of the devil, and setteth us at liberty.

2. 48. But remember he is the God of mercy and of truth, and cannot but fulfil his promises. Also remember, that his Son's blood is stronger than all the sins and wickedness of the whole world; and therewith quiet thyself, and thereunto commit thyself, and bless thyself in all temptation (namely at the hour of death) with that holy candle.

3. 55. And whensoever an occasion is given, he worketh naturally the will of God: for this blessing is given to all them that trust in Christ's blood, that they thirst and hunger to do God's will.

4. 63. The cause is: forasmuch as faith justifieth and putteth away sin in the sight of God; bringeth life, health, and the favour of God; maketh us the heirs of God; poureth the Spirit of God into our souls; and filleth us with all godly fulness in Christ; it were too great a shame, rebuke and wrong unto the faith, yea, to Christ's blood, if a man would work anything to purchase that, wherewith faith hath endued him already, and God hath given him freely: . . .

5. 65. So now thou seest that life eternal and all good things are promised unto faith and belief; so that he that believeth on Christ shall be safe. Christ's blood hath purchased life for us, and hath made us the heirs of God; so that heaven cometh by Christ's blood. If thou wouldest obtain heaven with the merits and deservings of thine own works, so didst thou wrong, yea, and shamedst, the blood of Christ; and unto thee were Christ dead in vain.

6. 65f. So let thine eye be single, and look unto good living only, and take no thought for the reward, but be content: forasmuch as thou knowest and art sure, that the reward, and all things contained in God's promises, follow good living naturally; and thy good works do but testify only, and certify thee that the Spirit of God is in thee, whom thou hast received for an earnest of God's truth; and certify thee that the Spirit of God is in thee, whom thou hast received for an earnest of God's truth; and that thou art heir of all the goodness of God, and that all good things are thine already, purchased by Christ's blood.

7. 71. I cannot receive it of favour and of the bounties of God, freely, and by deserving of deeds also. But believe as the gospel, glad tidings and promises of God say unto thee; that for Christ's blood sake only, though faith, God is at one with thee, and thou received to mercy, and art become the son of God, and heir annexed with Christ of all the goodness of God; the earnest whereof is the Spirit of God poured into our hearts.

8. 71. Now is it Christ's blood only that deserveth all the promises of God.

9. 72. Christ's blood only putteth away all the sin that ever was, is, or shall be, from them that are elect and repent, believing the gospel, that is to say, God's promises in Christ.

10. 72. Not that our works make us the sons of God, but testify only, and certify our consciences, that we are the sons of God; and that God hath chosen us, and washed us in Christ's blood; and hath put his Spirit in us.

11. 72. But and if ye counterfeit and follow God in well doing, then no doubt it is a sign that the Spirit of God is in you, and also the favour of God, which is not in the world; and that ye are inheritors of all the promises of God, and elect unto the fellowship of the blood of Christ.

12. 73. This putteth us in remembrance of our duty, and sheweth what followeth good works; not that works deserve it, but that the reward is laid up for us in store, and we thereunto elect through Christ's blood, which the works testify.

13. 75. Then he mourneth in his heart, because he is in such bondage that he cannot do the will of God; and is an hungred and athirst after righteousness; for righteousness (I mean) which springeth out of Christ's blood, for strength to do the will of God; and turneth himself to the promises of God, and desireth him for his great mercy and truth, and for the blood of his Son Christ, to fulfil his promises, and to give him strength.

14. 76. To see inwardly that the law of God is so spiritual, that no flesh can fulfil it; and then for to mourn and sorrow, and to desire, yea, to hunger and thirst after strength to do the will of God from the ground of the heart, and (notwithstanding all the subtilty of the devil, weakness and feebleness of the flesh, and wondering of the world,) to cleave yet to the promises of God, and to believe that for Christ's blood sake thou art received to the inheritance of eternal life, is a wonderful thing, and a thing that the world

knoweth not of; but whosoever feeleth that, though he fall a thousand times in a day, doth yet rise a thousand times, and is sure that the mercy of God is upon him.

15. 76. If I forgive, God shall forgive me; not for my deed's sake, but for his promises' sake, for his mercy and truth, and for the blood of his Son, Christ our Lord. And my forgiving certifieth my spirit that God shall forgive me, yea, that he hath forgiven me already.

16. 77. Have an eye to good works, to which if ye have lust and also power to do them, then are ye sure that the Spirit of God is in you, and ye in Christ elect to the reward of eternal life, which followeth good works. But look that thine eye be single, and rob not Christ of his honour; ascribe not that to the deserving of thy works, which is given thee freely by the merits of his blood. In Christ we are sons. In Christ we are heirs. In Christ God chose us, and elected us before the beginning of the world, created us anew by the word of the gospel, and put his Spirit in us, for because that we should do good works.

17. 78. For it followeth, "He that heareth the word, and doth it, buildeth his house upon a rock," and no tempest of temptations can overthrow it. For the Spirit of God is in his heart, and comforteth him, and holdeth him fast to the rock of the merits of Christ's blood, in whom he is elect.

18. 80. Now he that receiveth a prophet, a just man, or a disciple, shall have the same or like reward; that is to say, shall have the same eternal life which is appointed for them in Christ's blood and merits. For except thou were elect to the same eternal life, and hadst the same faith and trust in God, and the same Spirit, thou couldst never consent to their deeds and help them.

19. 82f. Thou readest in the text, that the kingdom was "prepared for us from the beginning of the world." And we are blessed and sanctified. In Christ's blood are we blessed from that bitter curse and damnable captivity under sin, wherein we were born and conceived. And Christ's Spirit is poured into us, to bring forth good works, and our works are the fruits of the Spirit; and the kingdom is he deserving of Christ's blood; and so is faith, and the Spirit, and good works also.

20. 85. "This do and thou shalt live." Luke x. That is to say, "Love thy Lord God with all thy heart, with all thy soul, and with all thy strength, and with all thy mind; and thy neighbour as thyself." As who should say, If thou do this, or though thou canst not do it, yet if thou feelest lust thereunto, and thy spirit sigheth, mourneth, and longeth after strength to do it, take a sign and evident token thereby, that the Spirit of life is in thee, and that thou art elect to life everlasting by Christ's blood, whose gift and purchase is thy faith, and that Spirit that worketh the will of God in thee; whose gift also are thy deeds, or rather the deeds of the Spirit of Christ, and not thine; and whose gift is the reward of eternal life, which followeth good works.

21. 86. In the law may neither Peter nor Paul nor any other creature, save Christ only, rejoice. In the blood of Christ, which fulfilled the law for us, may every person that repenteth, believeth, loveth the law, and mourneth for strength to fulfil it, rejoice, be he never so weak a sinner.

22. 92. All those men fast without conscience of God, and without knowledge of the true intent of fasting, and do no other than honour saints, as the Gentiles and heathen worship their idols, and are drowned in blindness, and know not of the testament that God hath made to man-ward in Christ's blood. In God have they neither hope nor confidence, neither believe his promises, neither know his will, but are yet in captivity under the prince of darkness.

23. 93. The spirit waiteth and watcheth on the will of God, and ever hath her own fragility and weakness before her eyes; and when she seeth temptation and peril draw nigh, she turneth to God, and to the testament that God hath made to all that believe and trust in Christ's blood; and desireth God for his mercy and truth, and for the love he hath to Christ, that he will fulfil his promise, and that he will succour, and help, and give us strength, and that he will sanctify is name in us, and fulfil his godly will in us, and that he will not look on our sin and iniquity, but on his mercy, on his truth, and on the love that he oweth to his Son Christ; . . .

24. 93f. And whensoever he seeth occasion, he cannot but pray for his neighbour as well as for himself: his nature is to seek the honour of God in all men, and to draw (as much as in him is) all men unto God. This is the law of love, which springeth out of Christ's blood into the hearts of all them that have their trust in him.

25. 94. God, for his truth's sake, must put the righteousness of Christ in him, and wash his unrighteousness away in the blood of Christ.

26. 94. His heart sinneth not, but mourneth, repenteth, and consenteth unto the law and will of God, and justifieth God; that is, beareth record that God which made the law is righteous and just. And such an heart, trusting is Christ's blood, is accepted for full righteous. And his weakness, infirmity, and frailty is pardoned, and his sins not looked upon, until God put more strength in him, and fulfil his lust.

27. 95. And God hath promised, that whosoever calleth on his name shall never be confounded or ashamed. If the righteous fall (saith the scripture), he shall not be bruised; the Lord shall put his hand under him. Who is righteous but he that trusteth in Christ's blood, be he never so weak? Christ is our righteousness; and in him ought we to teach all men to trust; and to expound unto all men the testament that God hath made to us sinners in Christ's blood.

28. 96f. This order useth Paul in all his epistles: first, he preacheth the law, and proveth that the whole nature of man is damned, in that the heart lusteth

contrary to the will of God. For if we were of God, no doubt we should
have lust in his will. Then preacheth he Christ, the gospel, the promises,
and the mercy that God hath set forth to all men in Christ's blood: which
they that believe, and take it for an earnest thing, turn themselves to God,
begin to love God again, and to prepare themselves to his will, by the
working of the Spirit of God in them.

29. 97f. A Christian man hath nought to rejoice in, as concerning his deeds.
His rejoicing is that Christ died for him, and that he is washed in Christ's
blood. Of his deeds rejoiceth he not, neither counteth he his merits, neither
giveth pardons of them, neither seeketh an higher place in heaven of them,
neither maketh himself a saviour of other men through his good works: but
giveth all honour to God; and in his greatest deeds of mercy knowledgeth
himself sinner unfeignedly, . . .

30. 100. He that seeketh with his alms more than to be merciful to a neighbour,
to succour his brother's need, to do his duty to his brother, to give his
brother that he oweth him, the same is blind, and seeth not what it is to be
a Christian man, and to have fellowship in Christ's blood.

31. 107. But and we be merciful to the poor, for conscience to God, and of
compassion and hearty love, which compassion and love spring of the love
we have to God in Christ, for the pure mercy and love that he hath shewed
on us: then have we a sure token that we are beloved of God, and washed
in Christ's blood, and elect, by Christ's deserving, unto eternal life.

32. 108. If thou shouldest say (as saith John, the ivth of his epistle), "How can
he that loveth not his neighbour whom he seeth, love God whom he seeth
not?" Aristotle would say, Lo, a man must first love his neighbour and
then God; and out of the love to thy neighbour springeth the love to God.
But he that feeleth the working of the Spirit of God, and also from what
vengeance the blood of Christ hath delivered him, understandeth how that
it is impossible to love either father or mother, sister, brother, neighbour, or
his own self aright, except it spring out of the love to God; and perceiveth
that the love to a man's neighbour is a sign of the love to God, as good fruit
declareth a good tree.

33. 109. Moreover, when he saith, he shall receive much more in this world, of
a truth, yea, he hath received much more already. For except he had felt the
infinite mercy, goodness, love, and kindness of God, and the fellowship of
the blood of Christ, and the comfort of the Spirit of Christ in his heart, he
could never have forsaken any thing for God's sake.

34. 110. John i.; that is, God's favour was so full in Christ, that for his sake
he giveth us his favour, as affirmeth also Paul, Eph. i., "He loved us in his
beloved, by whom we have," saith Paul, "redemption through his blood,
and forgiveness of sins." The forgiveness of sins, then, is our redemption
in Christ, and not the reward of works.

35. 113f. Moreover, if the reward should depend and hang of the works, no man should be saved: forasmuch as our best deeds, compared to the law, are damnable sin. "By the deeds of the law is no flesh justified," as it is written in the third chapter to the Romans. The law justifieth not, but uttereth the sin only; and compelleth and driveth the penitent, or repenting sinner, to flee unto the sanctuary of mercy in the blood of Christ.

36. 117. Now ought not the cruelness and churlishness of father and mother, of husband, master, lord, or king, cause us to hate the commandment of our so kind a Lord, Christ; which spared not his blood for our sakes; which also hath purchased for us with his blood the reward of eternal life; which life shall follow the patience of good living, and whereunto our good deeds testify that we are chosen.

37. 122. Moreover, how many hundred thousand are there, which when they have sinned, and knowledge their sins, yet trust in a bald ceremony, or in a lousy friar's coat and merits; or in the prayers of them that devour widows' houses, and eat the poor out of house and harbour; in a thing of his own imagination; in a foolish dream, and a false vision; and not in Christ's blood, and in the truth that God hath sworn!

38. 125. Thus seest thou that James, when he saith, "Faith without deeds is dead," and, "as the body without the spirit is dead, so is faith without deeds," and, "the devils believe;" that he meaneth not of the faith and trust, that we have in the truth of God's promises, and his holy testament made unto us in Christ's blood; which faith followeth repentance, and the consent of the heart unto the law of God, and maketh a man safe, and setteth him at peace with God.

39. 125. For how can they believe that Christ died for their sins, and that he is their only and sufficient Saviour, seeing that they seek other saviours of their own imagination; and seeing that they feel not their sins, neither repent, except that some repent (as I above said) for fear of pain, but for no love, nor consent unto the law of God, nor longing that they have for those good promises which he hath made them in Christ's blood?

Obedience – Blood (PS-1)

1. 184. In like manner is it for the most part of our most holy religions. For they of like imagination do things which they of Bedlam may see that they are but madness. They look on the miracles which God did by the saints, to move the unbelieving unto the faith, and to confirm the truth of his promises in Christ, whereby all that believe are made saints; as thou seest in the last chapter of Mark. "They preached," saith he, "every where, the Lord working with them, and confirming their teaching with miracles that followed." . . . See what miracles God hath shewed for this saint; he must be verily great with God! – and at once they turn themselves from

God's word, and put their trust and confidence in the saint and his merits; and make an advocate, or rather a god of the saint; and of their blind imagination make a testament, or bond, between the saint and them, the testament of Christ's blood clean forgotten.

2.   202. Let kings, if they had lever be Christian in deed than so to be called, give themselves altogether to the wealth of their realms after the ensample of Christ; remembering that the people are God's, and not theirs; yea, are Christ's inheritance and possession, bought with his blood.

3.   213. The gospel is every where one, though it be preached of divers, and signifieth glad tidings: that is to wit, an open preaching of Christ, and the holy testament and gracious promises that God hath made in Christ's blood to all that repent and believe.

4.   227. Yea, and when a novice of the Observants is professed, the father asketh him, Will ye keep the rules of holy St. Francis? and he saith, Yea. Will ye so in deed? saith he. The other answereth, Yea, forsooth, father. Then saith the father, And I promise you again everlasting life. O blasphemy! If eternal life be due unto the pilled traditions of lousy friars, where is the testament become that God made unto us in Christ's blood? Christ saith, 'That there shall come pseudo-Christi;' which though I, for a consideration, have translated false Christ's, keeping the Greek word, yet signifieth it in the English, 'false anointed,' and ought so to be translated.

5.   228. For sin we through fragility never so oft, yet as soon as we repent and come into the right way again, and unto the testament that God hath made in Christ's blood, our sins vanish away as smoke in the wind, and as darkness at the coming of light; or as thou castest a little blood, or milk, into the main sea: insomuch as whosoever goeth about to make satisfaction for his sins to God-ward, saying in his heart, This much have I sinned, this much will I do again; or this-wise will I live to make amends withal; or this will I do, to get heaven withal; the same is an infidel, faithless, and damned in his deed-doing, and hath lost his part in Christ's blood; because he is disobedient unto God's testament, and setteth up another of his own imagination, unto which he will compel God to obey.

6.   240, If he believe in Christ, then is he a member of Christ, Christ's brother, Christ's flesh, Christ's blood, Christ's spouse, coheir with Christ, and hath his Spirit in earnest, and is also spiritual.

7.   246f. [Commenting on the hierarchy of the Church.] Behold how they are esteemed, and how high they be crept up above all; not into worldly seats only, but into the seat of God, the hearts of men, where they sit above God himself. For both they, and whatsoever they make of their own heads, is more feared and dread than God and his commandments. In them and their deservings put we more trust than in Christ and his merits. To their promises give we more faith than to the promises which God hath sworn in Christ's blood.

8. 251. Whatsoever false sign they make of them, I care not; but of this I am sure, that as the old hypocrites, when they had slain Christ, set poleaxes to keep him in his sepulchre, that he should not rise again, even so have our hypocrites buried the testament that God made unto us in Christ's blood; and to keep it down, that it rise not again, is all their study; whereof these poleaxes are the very sign.

9. 252f. So the sacrament of the body and blood of Christ hath a promise annexed, which the priest should declare in the English tongue. "This is my body, that is broken for you." "This is my blood, that is shed for many, unto the forgiveness of sins." "This do in remembrance of me," saith Christ, Luke xxii. And 1 Cor. xi. If when thou seest the sacrament, or eatest his body, or drinkest his blood, thou have this promise fast in thine heart, that his body was slain and his blood shed for thy sins, and believest it, so art thou saved and justified thereby.

10. 253. The washing [baptism] preacheth unto us. that we are cleansed with Christ's blood-shedding; which was an offering, and a satisfaction, for the sin of all that repent and believe, consenting and submitting themselves unto the will of God.

11. 262f. This confession is necessary all our lives long, as is repentance. And as thou understandest of repentance, so understand of this confession; for it is likewise included in the sacrament of baptism. For we always repent, and always knowledge or confess our sins unto God, and yet despair not; but remember that we are washed in Christ's blood: which thing our baptism doth represent and signify unto us.

12. 278. The sacrament of Christ's body after thiswise preach they. Thou must believe that it is no more bread, but the very body of Christ, flesh, blood and bone, even as he went here on earth, save his coat: for that is here yet; I wot not in how many places.

13. 278. We have a promise that Christ, and his body, and his blood, and all that he did, and suffered, is a sacrifice, a ransom, and a full satisfaction for our sins; that God for his sake will think no more on them, if we have power to repent and believe.

14. 280. To pray for one another are we equally bound, and to pray is a thing that we may always do, whatsoever we have in hand; and that to do may no man hire another, Christ's blood hath hired us already.

15. 284f. They preach also, that the wagging of the bishop's hand over us blesseth us, and putteth away our sins. Are these works not against Christ? How can they do more shame unto Christ's blood? . . . Thou wilt say: When we come first to the faith, then Christ forgiveth us and blesseth us; but the sins, which we afterward commit, are forgiven us through such things. I answer, if any man repent truly, and come to the faith, and put his trust in Christ, then as oft as he sinneth of frailty, at the sigh of the heart

is his sin put away in Christ's blood. For Christ's blood purgeth ever and blesseth ever. For John saith in the second of his first Epistle, "This I write unto you that ye sin not. And though any man sin" (meaning of frailty, and so repent) "yet have we an Advocate with the Father, Jesus Christ which is righteous, and he it is that obtaineth grace for our sins."

16. 288. Paul, Peter, and all true apostles preached Christ only. And the miracles did but confirm and stablish their preaching, and those everlasting promises and eternal testament that God had made between man and him in Christ's blood: and the miracles did testify also that they were true servants of Christ.

17. 292. God hath also made us promises, and hath sworn; yea, hath made a testament or a covenant, and hath bound himself, and hath sealed his obligation with Christ's blood, and confirmed it with miracles.

18. 292. When they say, 'We be sinners:' I answer, that Christ is no sinner, save a satisfaction and an offering for sin. Take Christ from the saints, and what are they? What is Paul without Christ? Is he anything save a blasphemer, a persecutor, a murderer, and a shedder of christian blood? But as soon as he came to Christ, he was no more a sinner, but a minister of righteousness.

19. 294f. It followeth, "God setteth out his love, that he hath to us;" (that is, he maketh it appear, that men may perceive love if they be not more than stock blind;) "inasmuch (saith Paul) as, while we were yet sinners, Christ died for us. Much more now, (saith he,) seeing we are justified by his blood, shall we be preserved from wrath through him: for if when we were enemies, we were reconciled to God by the death of his Son; much more, seeing we are reconciled, we shall be preserved by his life."

20. 296. We are all the sons of God, all Christ's servants bought with his blood; and every man to other Christ his own self.

21. 299. Thus is God in Christ all in all; good and bad receive I of God. Them that are good I love, because they are in Christ; and the evil, to bring them to Christ. When any man doth well, I rejoice that God is honoured; and when any man doth evil, I sorrow because that God is dishonoured. Finally, inasmuch as God hath created all, and Christ bought all with his blood, therefore ought all to seek God and Christ in all, and else nothing.

22. 325. And when they cry, 'Miracles, miracles,' remember that God hath made an everlasting testament with us in Christ's blood, against which we may receive no miracles.

23. 329. And when the friars say, they do more than their duty when they preach, and more than they are bound to: ('To say our service are we bound, say they, and that is our duty; and to preach is more than we are bound to:) set thou before thee how that Christ's blood-shedding hath bound us to love one another with all our might, and to do the uttermost

of our power one to another. And Paul saith, 1 Cor. ix. "Woe be unto me, if I preach not:" yea, woe is unto him that hath wherewith to help his neighbour, and to make him better, and do it not.

24. 334. In Christ we are all one, and even brethren. No man is his own; but we are all Christ's servants, bought with Christ's blood. Therefore ought no man to seek himself, or his own profit, but Christ and his will.

25. 334. We also serve, not as servants unto masters; but as they which are bought with Christ's blood serve Christ himself. We be here all servants unto Christ. For whatsoever we do one to another in Christ's name, that do we unto Christ, and the reward of that shall we receive of Christ.

26. 339. Sent not the pope also unto the king of France remission of his sins, to go and conquer King John's realm? So now remission of sins cometh not by faith in the testament that God hath made in Christ's blood, but by fighting and murdering for the pope's pleasure.

27. 340. A Christian man is the temple of God and of the Holy Ghost, and hallowed in Christ's blood. A Christian man is holy in himself, by reason of the Spirit that dwelleth in him; and the place wherein he is, is holy by reason of him, whether he be in the field or town.

Exposition of Matthew V, Vi, Vii (**PS-2**)

1. 4f. Now if thou give the law a false gloss, and say that the law is a thing which a man may do of his own strength, even out of the power of his free-will; and that by the deeds of the law thou mayest deserve the forgiveness of thy fore sins; then died Christ in vain, and is made almost of no stead, seeing thou art become thine own saviour. Neither can Christ (where that gloss is admitted) be otherwise taken or esteemed of Christian men, for all his passion and promises made to us in his blood, than he is of the Turks: . . .

2. 6. Another conclusion is this: all the good promises which are made us throughout all the scripture, for Christ's sake, for his love, his passion or suffering, his blood-shedding or death, are all made us on this condition and covenant on our party, that we henceforth love the law of God, to walk therein, and to do it, and fashion our lives thereafter: insomuch that whosoever hath not the law of God written in his heart, that he love it, have his lust in it, and record therein night and day, understanding it as God hath given it, and as Christ and the apostles expound it., the same hath no part in the promises, nor can have any true faith in the blood of Christ; because there is no promise made him, but to them only that promise to keep the law.

3. 10. Of this ye see the difference between the sin of them that believe in the blood of Christ for the remission of sin, and consent and submit themselves

unto the law, and the sin of them that yield themselves unto sin, to serve it, &c. The first sin under grace; and their sins are venial, that is to say, forgiveable.

4.   10. Of this also ye see the difference between the lambs of true believers; and between the unclean swine, that follow carnal lusts and fleshly liberty; and the churlish and hypocritish dogs, which, for the blind zeal of their own righteousness, persecute the righteousness of the faith in Christ's blood. The effeminate and careless swine, which continue in their fleshliness, and cease not to wallow themselves in their old puddle, think that the believe very well in Christ's blood; but they are deceived; as thou mayest clearly perceive, because they fear not the damnation of evil works, nor love the law of good works, and therefore have no part in the promise.

5.   11. Ye see also the difference of all manner of faiths. The faith of the true believers is, that God justifieth or forgiveth; and Christ deserveth it; and the faith or trust in Christ's blood receiveth it, and certifieth the conscience thereof, and saveth and delivereth her from fear of death and damnation. And this is that we mean, when we say faith justifieth: that faith (I mean in Christ, and not in our own works) certifieth the conscience that our sins are forgiven us for Christ's blood's sake.

6.   11. And thus ye see that faith is the thing that is affirmed to justify, of all parties. For faith in Christ's blood (which is God's promise) quieteth the conscience of the true believers: and a false faith, or trust in works (which is their own feigning), beguileth the blind hypocrites for a season; . . .

7.   11f. Another conclusion is this: to believe in Christ for the remission of sins, and, of a thankfulness for that mercy, to love the law truly: that is to say, to love God that is the Father of all and giveth all; and Jesus Christ, that is Lord of us all, and bought us all, with all our hearts, souls, power, and might; and our brethren for our Father's sake (because they be created after his image), and for our Lord and master Christ's sake, because they be the price of his blood; and to long for the life to come, because this life cannot be led without sin. These three points (I say) are the profession and religion of a Christian man, and the inward baptism of the heart, signified by the outward washing of the body. And they be that spiritual character, badge, or sign, wherewith God, through his Spirit, marketh all his immediately and as soon as they be joined to Christ, and made members of his church by true faith.

8.   12. For when they come to the point, that they should minister Christ's passion unto the salvation of our souls, there they poison altogether and gloss out the law, that should make us feel our salvation in Christ, and drive us in that point from Christ, and teach us to put our trust in our own works for the remission and satisfaction of our sins, and in the apish play of hypocrites, which sell their merits instead of Christ's blood and passion.

9.   13. Lo, now, dear reader, to believe in Christ's blood for the remission of sin, and purchasing of all the good promises that help to the life to come; and to love the law; and to long for the life to come, is the inward baptism of the soul, the baptism that only availeth in the sight of God; the new generation and image of Christ; the only key also to bind and to loose sinners; . . .

10.   13. And though faith in Christ's blood make the marriage between our soul and Christ, and is properly the marriage garment; yea, and the sign Thau, that defendeth us from the smiting and power of the evil angels; and is also the rock whereon Christ's church is built, and whereon all that is built standeth against all weather of wind and tempests; yet might the profession of the faith in Christ's blood, and of the love to the law, and longing for the life to come, be called all these things, were malice and froward understanding away; because that where one of them is, there will be all three; and where all are not, there is none of them.

11.   15. Go to then, and desire God to print this profession in thine heart, and to increase it daily more and more; that thou mayest be full shapen like unto the image of Christ, in knowledge and love, and meek thyself, and creep low by the ground, and cleave fast to the rock of this profession, and tie to thy ship this anchor of faith in Christ's blood with the cable of love, to cast it out against all tempests; and so set up thy sail, and get thee to the main sea of God's word.

12.   17. And contrariwise, unhappy and accursed, and that with the first and deepest of all curses, are the rich in spirit; that is to say, the covetous that, being rich, trust in their riches, or, being poor, long for the consolation of riches; and comfort not their souls with the promises of their heavenly Father, confirmed with the blood of their Lord Christ.

13.   29, Here seest thou the uttermost, what a Christian must look for. It is not enough to suffer for righteousness; but that no bitterness or poison be left out of thy cup, thou shalt be reviled and railed upon; and even when thou art condemned to death, then be excommunicate and delivered to Satan, deprived of the fellowship of holy church, the company of the angels, and of thy part in Christ's blood; and shalt be cursed down to hell, defied, detested, and execrate with all the blasphemous railings that the poisonful heart of hypocrites can think or imagine.

14.   33. "If salt have lost his saltness, it is good for nothing but to be trodden under foot of men." That is, if the preacher, which for his doctrine is called salt, have lost the nature of salt, that is to say, his sharpness in rebuking all unrighteousness, all natural reason, natural wit and understanding, and all trust and confidence in whatsoever it be, save in the blood of Christ; he is condemned of God, and disallowed of all them that cleave to the truth.

15. 34. What true Christian man can give honour to that that taketh all honour from Christ? Who can give honour to that that slayeth the soul of his brother, and robbeth his heart of that trust and confidence, which he should give to his Lord that hath bought him with his blood.

16. 34. Whatsoever holiness, wisdom, virtue, perfectness, or righteousness, is in the world among men, howsoever perfect and holy they appear; yet is all damnable darkness, except the right knowledge of Christ's blood be there first, to justify the heart, before all other holiness.

17. 36, May I then, and ought also, to resist father and mother and all temporal power with God's word, when they wrongfully do or command that hurteth or killeth the body; and have I no power to resist the bishop or preacher, that with false doctrine slayeth the souls, for which my master and Lord Christ hath shed his blood?

18. 55f. Now if truth be not in thy words, thou shamest thine heavenly Father, and testifiest that thou believest that he is no righteous judge, nor will avenge unrighteousness; but that he is wicked as thou art, and consenteth and laugheth at thee, while thou deceivest thy brother, as well created after the likeness of God, and as dear bought with the precious blood of Christ, as thou.

19. 62. Concerning thyself, oppress not thy subjects with rent, fines, or custom at all, neither pill them with taxes and such like, to maintain thine own lusts; but be loving and kind to them, as Christ was to thee; for they be his, and the price of his blood.

20. 63. And like is it, if thy lord or prince send thee a warfare into another land; thou must obey at God's commandment, and go, and avenge thy prince's quarrel, which thou knowest not but that it is right. And when thou comest thither, remember what thou art in the first state with them against whom thou must fight, how that they be thy brethren, and as deeply bought with Christ's blood as thou, and for Christ's sake to be beloved in thine heart.

21. 64. Now concerning the goods of this world, it is easy to judge. In the first state or degree thou oughtest to be thankful to Christ, and to love, to give, and to lend to them that are bought with his precious blood, all that thou art able. For all that thou owest to Christ, whose servant thou art to do his will, that must [thou] pay them.

22. 68f. Concerning lending, proceed by the foresaid rule of mercy. Many, in extreme need, yet ashamed to beg, shall desire thee to lend. Unto such, instead of ending, give; or say thus, 'Lo, here is as much as you require. If ye can pay it again well, do, and ye shall find me ready against another time, to lend or give (if need be) as much more. But and if ye shall not be able to pay it again, trouble not your conscience, I give it you. We be all one man's children: one man hath bought us all with his blood, and bound us to help one another.' And with so doing thou shalt win the heart of him to thy Father.

23. 76. And as touching forgiveness of sin: though forgiveness of sin be promised unto thee, yet challenge it not by thy merits, but by the merits of Christ's blood; and hear what Paul saith: . . .

24. 87. Furthermore, though forgiveness of thy sins be annexed to thy work and forgiving thy brother; yet do not (as I said) thy works justify thee before God. But the faith in Christ's blood, and in the promises made to us for his sake, doth bring righteousness into the heart. And the righteousness of the heart by faith is felt and known by the work: as Peter in the first of his second epistle, commandeth to do good works, for to make our vocation and election sure; that we might feel our faith, and be certified that it is right.

25. 88f. This is then the sum of all together: works are the outward righteousness before the world, and may be called the righteousness of the members, and spring of inward love. Love is the righteousness of the heart, and springeth of faith. Faith is the trust in Christ's blood, and is the gift of God; whereunto a man is drawn of the goodness of God, and driven through true knowledge of the law, and of beholding his deeds in the lust and desire of the members unto the request of the law, . . .

26. 89. And when I say faith justifieth, the understanding is, that faith receiveth the justifying. God promiseth to forgive us our sins, and to impute us for full righteous. And God justifieth us actively: that is to say, forgiveth us, and reckoneth us for full righteous. And Christ's blood deserveth it; and faith in the promise receiveth it, and certifieth the conscience thereof.

27. 96. If thou love and pity thy neighbour, and help him, thy alms is acceptable. If thou do it of vain-glory, to have the praise that belongeth to God, or for a greater, profit only, or to make satisfaction for thy sins past, and to dishonour Christ's blood, which hath made it already; then is thine alms abominable. If thy prayer be thanks in heart, or calling to God for help, with trust in him according to his promise, then thy prayer pleaseth. If thou believe in Christ's blood for the remission of sins, and henceforth hatest sin, that thou punishest thy body to slay thy lusts, and to keep them under, that thou sin not again; then it pleaseth God exceedingly.

28. 97f. And as for the hypocrisy of the fratry, where they eat but invisible flesh, or that is interpret to be no flesh, [it] is spoken of in other places. Another proof is that they so long a time have given pardons, of the merits of their fasting, as though they had done more than enough for themselves; and of that merchandise have gotten all they have, and have brought the knowledge of Christ's blood clean into darkness.

29. 103. How dark is the doctrine of them that teach that a man may compel God, with the works of free-will, to give him his favour and grace; or make God unrighteous! How dark is the doctrine of them which (to the rebuke of Christ's blood) teach that works do justify before God, and

make satisfaction for sins! How blind are they which think prayer to be the pattering of many words; and will therefore not only be praised and paid of the world, but also by the title thereof challenge heaven, and not by the merits of Christ's blood.

30. 108. The kingdom of God is the gospel and doctrine of Christ. And the righteousness thereof is to believe in Christ's blood, for the remission of sins: out of which righteousness springeth love to God, and thy neighbour, for his sake; which is also righteousness, as I have said afore, so far as it is perfect, and that which lacketh is supplied by faith in God's word, in that he has promised to accept that, till more come.

31. 109. And these have our spiritualty with their corrupt doctrine mingled together, (that is to say, the righteousness of the kingdom of God, which is faith in Christ's blood, and the outward righteousness of the members,) that we ascribe to the one that pertaineth to the other.

32. 116. Christ warned his disciples at his last supper, to have peace in him; affirming that they should have none in the world. The false prophets shall ever impugn the faith in Christ's blood, and enforce to quench the true understanding of the law, and the right meaning and intent of all the works commanded by God; which fight is a fight above all fights.

33. 122f. They have robbed Christ of all his merits, and clothed themselves therewith. They have robbed the soul of man of the bread of her life, the faith and trust in Christ's blood; and have fed her with the shales and cods of the hope in their merits and confidence in their good works.

34. 126. If a king minister his kingdom in the faith of this name, because his subjects be his brethren and the price of Christ's blood, he pleaseth God highly; and if this faith be not there, it pleaseth him not. And if I sew a shoe truly, in the faith of his name, to do my brother service, because he is the price of Christ's blood, it pleaseth God. Thus is faith the goodness of all works.

35. 130f. And upon that they consent to the law, love it, and profess it, to fulfil it to the uttermost of their power, and then go to and work. Faith, or confidence in Christ's blood, without help, and before the works of the law, bringeth all manner of remission of sins, and satisfaction. Faith is mother of love; faith accompanieth love in all her works, to fulfil as much as there lacketh, in our doing the law, of that perfect love which Christ had to his Father and us, in his fulfilling of the law for us.

Exposition of the First Epistle of Saint John (PS-2)

1. 136f. And to have this profession written in thine heart is to consent unto the law that it is righteous and good, and to love it in thine heart, and to submit thyself thereunto for to learn it, and to rule and square all thy deeds

thereby; and then to believe in Christ, that for his sake all thy sins, which thou diddest before the knowledge of this profession, are forgiven thee clearly, both *a pœna et culpa,* to use the Romish terms; and that for none other satisfaction to God-ward than Christ's blood; and even so, that all the sin which we do after this knowledge, either of chance. Ignorance, infirmity, negligence, or provoked and overcome of the flesh, is forgiven us likewise, both *pœna et culpa,* through repentance and faith in Christ, without our satisfaction of works to God-ward.

2. 137. But to God-ward is there no satisfaction, save faith in Christ's blood out of a repenting heart.

3. 3. 140. *He that hath the profession of his baptism written in his heart can be no heretic.* And on the other side, they have utterly forsaken themselves, with all their high learning and wisdom, and are become the servants of Christ only, which hath bought them with his blood; and have promised in their hearts unfeignedly to follow him, and to take him only for the author of their religion, and his doctrine only for their wisdom and learning, and to maintain it in word and deed, and to keep it pure, and to build no strange doctrine thereupon, . . .

4. 4. 141. The whole sum then of all together is this: If our hearts were taught the appointment made between God and us in Christ's blood, when we were baptized, we had the key to open the scripture, and light to see and perceive the true meaning of it, and the scripture should be easy understand.

5. 145f. John i. "He gave them power to be the sons of God, in that they believed in his name;" and John iii., "He that believeth in the Son hath everlasting life;" and a little before in the said chapter, "He that believeth in him shall not be condemned." And to believe in the words of this article is that eating of Christ's flesh, and drinking his blood, of which is spoken, John vi. "The words that I speak are spirit and life, and the flesh profiteth not at all;" meaning of the fleshly eating of his body, and the fleshly drinking of is blood.

6. 146. But as he which feeleth not his disease can long for no health, even so it is impossible for any man to believe in Christ's blood, except Moses have had him first in cure, and with his law hath robbed him of his righteousness, and condemned him unto everlasting death, and have shewed him under what damnation they are in by birth in Adam, and how all their deeds (appear they never so holy) are yet but damnable sin, because they can refer nothing unto the glory of God, but seek themselves, their own profit, honour and glory: so that repentance toward the law must go before this belief; and he that repenteth not, but consenteth unto the life of sin, hath no part in this faith.

7. 149. And then, finally, if we have the light in our hearts, and walk therein, then have we fellowship with God, and are his sons and heirs, and are purged from all sin through Christ's blood.

8. 150. For he promised Abraham, that in his Seed all the world should be blessed from the curse of sin; and hath abundantly renewed his everlasting mercy unto us in the new Testament, promising that our sins shall be forgiven in Christ's blood, if we repent, and trust thereto.

9. 152. I write unto you on the one side, that God is light; and therefore that no man, which willingly walketh in the unfruitful works of darkness, hath any fellowship with that light, or part in the blood of his Son.

10. 152f. And besides that, our Jesus is God, and Almighty. He took our nature upon him, and felt all our infirmities and sicknesses, and in feeling learned to have compassion on us, and for compassion cried mightily in prayers to God the Father for us, and was heard. And the voice of the same blood that once cried, not for vengeance as Abel's, but for mercy only, and was heard, crieth now and ever, and is ever heard, as oft as we call unto remembrance with repenting faith, how that it was shed for our sins.

11. 154f. . . . that our Jesus, our Saviour, that saveth his people from their sins, and our Christ, that is our king over all sin, death and hell, anointed with fullness of all grace and with the Spirit of God, to distribute unto all men, hath, according unto the epistle to the Hebrews and all the scripture, in the days of his mortal flesh, with fasting, praying, suffering, and crying to God mightily for us, and with shedding his blood, made full satisfaction both *a pœna et culpa* (with our holy father's leave) for all the sins of the world; both of theirs that went before, and of theirs that come after in the faith; whether it be original sin or actual: and not only the sins committed with consent to evil in time of ignorance, before the knowledge of the truth, but also the sins done of frailty after we have forsaken evil and consented to the laws of God in our hearts, promising to follow Christ and to walk in the light of his doctrine.

12. 157. For it was a very strange speaking in Paul's ears, to call that grace that came of deserving of works; or that deserving of works which came by grace; for he reckoned works and grace to be contrary, in such manner of speech. But our holy father hath coupled them together, of pure liberality, I dare say, and not for covetousness. . . . even so of that blessed complexion he describeth the nature of the mercy of God, that God will remit his anger to us upon the appointment of our satisfaction: whereas the scripture saith, Christ is our righteousness, our justifying, our redemption, our atonement, that hath appeased God, and cleanseth us from our sins, and all in his blood, so that his blood is the satisfaction only.

13. 158. God's worship is to love him for his mercy; and of love to bestow all our works upon our neighbour for his sake, and upon the taming of our flesh, that we sin not again, which should be the chiefest care of a christian man; whilst Christ careth for that that is once past and committed already, whether before our profession or after. For the

conditions of the peace that is made between God and us in Christ's blood are these: The law is set before us, unto which if we consent and submit ourselves to be scholars thereof, then are not only all our fore sins forgiven, both *pœna et culpa,* (with our holy father's licence ever); but also all our infirmities, weakness, proneness, readiness, and motions unto sin, are pardoned, and taken aworth, and we translated from under the damnation of the law, ...

14. 160. Even so, whomsoever a true preacher of God's word saith shall be damned for his sin, because he will not repent and believe in Christ, the same is damned: and whomsoever a true preacher of God's word saith shall be saved, because he repenteth and believeth in Christ's blood, the same is saved. And this is the binding and loosing that Christ meant.

15. 160f. ... according to the profession of our baptism, which is the very sacrament or sign of repentance, (or, if they will so have it called, penance,) by the interpretation of Paul (Rom. vi.). For the plunging into the water, as it betokeneth on the one part that Christ hath washed our souls with his blood; even so on the other part it signifieth that we have promised to quench and slay the lusts of the flesh with prayer, fasting, and holy meditation, after the doctrine of Christ, and with all godly exercise, that tame the flesh, and kill not the man.

16. 162. And therefore the prelates, loath to lose their high authority, and to let the people go free of their yoke, began to turn their tale, and sing a new song, how that this penance was enjoined to make satisfaction to God for the sin that was committed; robbing our souls of the fruit of Christ's blood, and making us image-servants; referring our deeds unto the person of God, and worshipping him, as an image of our own imagination, with bodily work: saying moreover, if we would not do such penance here at their injunctions, we must do it in another world; and so feigned purgatory, where we must suffer seven years for every sin.

17. 162f. And the sacrament of penance they thus describe: contrition, confession, and satisfaction: contrition; sorrow for thy sins: confession; not to God and them whom thou hast offended, but tell thy sins in the priest's ear: satisfaction, to do certain deeds enjoined of them, to buy out thy sins. And in their description they have clean excluded the faith in the satisfaction of Christ's blood; which only bringeth life, and the spirit of life, and righteousness, and without the which it is impossible to please God: in whose stead they have put in the presumption of our own works. And for lack of trust in Christ's blood, our contrition is but a fruitless sorrow in the respect of hell, which maketh us hate the law still, and consequently God that made it: where true contrition, annexed with faith, is sorrow in respect of the law, unto which we consent that it is good, and love it, and therefore mourn, partly because we have offended it, and partly because we lack power to fulfil it as we would.

18. 163. And hereof ye may see how out of this open penance came the ear-confession, satisfaction of works, purgatory and pardons. For when they had put the satisfaction of Christ's blood out of the way, then as they compelled men to confess open sins, and to take open penance, even so they compelled them to confess secret sins, and to take secret penance. And as they made merchandise of open penance, so did they of secret.

19. 166. For first, God, which alone hath power to help or hurt, hath made appointment betwixt him and us, in Christ's blood; and hath bound himself to give us whatsoever we ask in his name, testifying thereto that there is no other name to be saved by; and that he will be a Father unto us, and save us both in this life and in the life to come, and take us from under the damnation of the law, and set us under grace and mercy, to be scholars only to learn the law; and that our unperfect deeds shall be taken in worth, yea, and though at a time we mar all through our infirmity, yet, if we turn again, that shall be forgiven us mercifully, so that we shall be under no damnation: which testament is confirmed with signs and wonders wrought through the Holy Ghost.

20. 167f. Moreover if the saints be in heaven, then can they be there in none other case than the angels; in which state Christ testifieth they shall be in the resurrection. Now the angels are ministers sent of God to do service unto the elect, which shall be saved. And God hath bound himself, that if I come in the right way, by the door of Christ's blood, and ask help, that he will send me, if need be, an hundred legions of angels or saints. . . . And therefore, when I appoint God whom he shall send, and bind him, where he hath not bound himself, to send me what saint I will, I tempt God. And thus this choosing of several saints is but tempting of God. And yet we do worse than this: for we leave the way of Christ's blood, and go not to God through him; but run to the saints, in a testament of our own making, and will that they either save us themselves for our image-service, or compel God for their merit's sake to save us.

21. 168. Why goest thou not unto thy Father thine ownself? 'I am a sinner,' will they say, 'and dare not.' If thou go in the right way, thou hast no sin. Christ hath taken all thy sins from thee; . . . But this way is stopped up through unbelief; and therefore we seek another, which is no way to life, but unto everlasting death. We will not look on the law with open eyes, and therefore have we no due repentance, and so no lust to hearken unto the gospel of glad tidings in Christ's blood. And where the right way is set before us, and we of malice will not walk therein, God cannot but let the devil play with us, and juggle our eyes to confirm us in blindness.

22. 172. The keeping of God's commandments certifieth us that we be in the state of grace. But our pharisaical doctors have no doctrine to know when a man is in a state of grace; . . . Neither know such doctors whether they be in state of grace, but keep men's commandments: . . . Though thou have

a devotion to stick up a candle before a post, and so forth yet thou canst never be sure thereby, that thou art in the favour of God. But if thou have devotion to help thy brother in all his misfortunes, because he is the image of God and price of Christ's blood, then thy devotion certifieth thee that thou art in the favour of God, or state of grace.

23. 181f. Verily, sir, the bishop of Rome seeketh himself, as all heretics did; and abuseth the name of Christ, to gather offerings, tithes and rents in his name, to bestow them unto his own honour and not Christ's, and the bring the conscience of the people into captivity under him through superstitions fear, as though he had such authority given him of Christ. . . . But all the texts that shew him to do his duty, he putteth out of the way; and all the texts thereto, that set the consciences at liberty in Christ, and prove our salvation to be in Christ only. And, with Pelagius, he preacheth the justifying of works; which is the denying of Christ. He preacheth a false binding and loosing with ear-confession, which is not in the trust and confidence of Christ's blood-shedding.

24. 182f. Nay, Christ is no hypocrite, or disguised, that playeth a part in a play, and representeth a person, or state, which he is not; but is always that his name signifieth, he is ever a Saviour, and ever anointeth with grace, and ever maketh God with us, and ever sanctifieth. Neither is there any other to save and sanctify from sin, or anoint with grace, or to set God at one with men. And these things, which his name signify, doth he ever unto all that have trust and confidence in his blood, as soon as they repent of the sin which they desire to be saved and sanctified from.

25. 183f. When a true preacher preacheth, the Spirit entereth into the hearts of the elect, and maketh them feel the righteousness of the law of God, and by the law the poison of their corrupt nature; and thence leadeth them, through repentance, unto the mercy that is in Christ's blood; and as an ointment healeth the body, even so the Spirit, through confidence and trust in Christ's blood, healeth the soul, and maketh her love the law of God; and therefore is it called anointing or an ointment, and may well be signified by the oil of our sacrament.

26. 187. The faith and hope of a Christian man are no dead, idle, or barren things; but lively, working, and fruitful. For when the law through conscience of sin hath slain the soul, then hope and trust in Christ's blood, through certifying of the conscience that the damnation of the law is taken away, quickeneth her again; and maketh her to love the law, which is the purifying of the soul, and her life, and serving the law in the inner man.

27. 188. But and if they will break into thy conscience, as the bishop of Rome doth with his dumb traditions, and saith, 'To do this saveth thy soul, and to leave it undone loseth thy soul;' then defy them as the works of antichrist, for they make thee sin against the faith that is in Christ's blood, by which

only thy soul is saved, and for lack of that only damned. And how love breaketh the law, take an example. It is a good law that men come to church on the Sundays, to hear God's word, and to receive the sacrament of the body and blood of Christ, in remembrance of his benefits, and so to strengthen thy soul for to walk in his love, and in the love of our neighbour for his sake, &c.: yet if my father, mother, or any other that requireth my help be sick, I break that good commandment, to do my duty to my elders or my neighbour.

28. 189. Whosoever preacheth Christ in word and deed, him take for Christ's vicar. And them that would prove themselves his vicars with sophistry, and when it is come to the point, make a sword only their mighty arguments, and live contrary to all his doctrine, and in all their preachings blaspheme and rail on his blessed blood, take for the vicars of antichrist.

29. 190. And Christ, which is contrary to the devil, came to destroy the works of the devil in us, and to give us a new birth, a new nature, and to sow new seed in us, that we should, by the reason of that birth, sin no more. For the seed of that birth, that is to wete the Spirit of God and the lively seed of his word sown in our hearts, keepeth our hearts, that we cannot consent to sin; as the seed of the devil holdeth the hearts of his, that they cannot consent to good. This is contrary unto the bishop of Rome in two points: in the one, that he saith, that our good deeds make us first good, and teacheth us not to believe in Christ's blood, there to be washed and made first good; and in another, that he saith, God chooseth us first for our good qualities and properties, and for the enforcement and good endeavour of our free-will.

30. 194. Thou shalt not know, by sprinkling thyself with holy water, nor kissing the pax, nor with taking ashes, or though thou were anointed with all the oil in Thames street, that thy faith is sure. But and if thou couldest find in thine heart to bestow both life and goods upon thy neighbour in a just cause, and hast proved it; then art thou sure, that thou lovest Christ, and feelest that thou hast thy trust in his blood.

31. 196. For the scripture testifieth that Christ hath taken away the sin of the world in his flesh; and that at the same hour that he yielded up his spirit into the hands of his Father, he had full purged, and made full satisfaction for all the sins of the world: so that all the sin of the world, both before his passion and after, must be put away through repentance toward the law, and faith and trust in his blood, without respect of any other satisfaction, sacrifice or work. For if I once sin, the law rebuketh my conscience, and setteth variance between God and me: and I shall never be at peace with God again, until I have heard the voice of his mouth, how that my sin is forgiven me for Christ's blood sake. And as soon as I believe that, I am at peace with God, and love his law again, and of love work.

32. 196. And that Christ hath done this service in his flesh, deny all the members of antichrist. And hereby shalt thou know them. All doctrine that

buildeth thee upon Christ to put thy trust and confidence in his blood, is of God, and true doctrine: and all doctrine that withdraweth thine hope and trust from Christ is of the devil, and the doctrine of antichrist.

33. 198. For the love of a man's neighbour unfeignedly springeth out of the unfeigned knowledge of God in Christ's blood: by which knowledge we be born of God, and love God and our neighbour for his sake. And so he that loveth his neighbour unfeignedly is sure of himself, that he knoweth God, and is of God unfeignedly: and contrariwise, he that loveth not, knoweth not God: for God in Christ's blood is such a love, that if a man saw it, it were impossible that he should not break out into the love of God again, and of his neighbour for his sake.

34. 199. If a man had once felt within his conscience the fierce wrath of God toward sinners, and the terrible and most cruel damnation that the law threateneth; and then beheld with the eyes of a strong faith the mercy, favour and grace, the taking away of the damnation of the law, and restoring again of life, freely offered us in Christ's blood, he should perceive love, and so much the more, that it was shewed us when we were sinners and enemies of God.

35. 200. If we felt the love of God in Christ's blood, we could not but love again, not only God and Christ, but also all that are bought with Christ's blood. If we love God for the pleasures that we receive, then love we ourselves. But if we love him to do him pleasure again; that can we no otherwise do, than in loving our neighbours for his sake; them that are good, to continue them in their goodness; and them that are evil, to draw them to good. . . . And therefore commandeth Christ, "Love your enemies, bless them that curse you, pray for them that persecute you, that ye may be the sons of your heavenly Father; which maketh his sun rise over good and bad, and sendeth his rain upon just and unjust:" yea, which made the sun of his mercy shine upon us, and sent the rain of the blood of his dear and only child upon our souls to quicken us, and to make us see love, to love again.

36. 207. The Spirit through faith certifieth my conscience that my sins are forgiven, and I received under grace, and made the very son of God, and beloved of God: and then naturally mine heart breaketh out into the love of God again, and I seek how to utter my love, and to do God some pleasure; and because I can neither do service nor pleasure unto his own person, my neighbour is set before me, to do God service and pleasure in him, and to be to him as Christ is to me, because he is my brother, bought with Christ's blood as I am.

37. 209f. Christ came with three witnesses, water, blood, and Spirit. He ordained the sacrament of baptism, to be his witness unto us. And he ordained the sacrament of his blood, to be his witness unto us. And he poureth his Spirit into the hearts of his, to testify and to make them feel that the testimony of these two sacraments are true. And the testimony of these three is, as it after followeth, that we have everlasting life in the Son of God.

38. 210. The true believers have the testimony of God in their hearts, and they glorify God, witnessing that he is true. They have the kingdom of God within them; and the temple of God within them; and God in that temple; and have the Son of God, and life through him. And in that temple they seek God, and offer for their sins the sacrifice of Christ's blood, and the fat of his mercies in the fire of their prayers; and in the confidence of that sacrifice go in boldly to God their Father.

39. 212. That they be neither bold nor sure, appeareth first by their deeds, and secondarily by their own confession; for they say, what should God hear them or grant them aught, seeing they be unworthy? yea, and they confirm it with a similitude of worldly wisdom, that they should be put back for their malapertness, and fare the worse; as if a rude fellow should break up into the king's privy chamber, and press unto his own person without knocking, or speaking to any other officer: so that they believe it an augmenting of sin to go to God themselves in the confidence of Christ's blood, as he bade them.

40. 215. The sacrifices of blood were ordained partly to be a secret prophesying of Christ's blood-shedding, and partly to be a testimony and certifying of our hearts, that the sin was forgiven, and peace made between us and God; and not to be a satisfaction: for that were image-service, and to make an image of God.

41. 217. St. White sendeth no rain upon the earth, nor maketh the sun shine thereon, nor maketh the grass grow. Neither is there any God's word that he will now do so much for us at her request. But God hath promised, if we will keep his laws, to do so much for us at our own request, for the blood of his Son Jesus.

42. 218. And this purchase made he with the things which he suffered in his flesh, and with the strong prayers which he prayed. And to keep his testament ever fresh in mind, that it were not forgotten, he left with us the sacrament or sign of his body and blood, to strength our faith, and to certify our conscience, that our sins were forgiven, as soon as we repented and had reconciled ourselves unto our brethren, and to arm our souls, through the continual remembrance of Christ's death, unto the despising of the world, mortifying of the flesh, and quenching of the lusts and thirsts of worldly things.

43. 220. [a summary of the communion service] And then the sacrament was ministered for the confirmation of the faith of the gospel, and of the testament made between God and us, of forgiveness of sins in Christ's blood for our repentance and faith; . . .

44. 221f. And of the very sacrament itself we know no other thing than that we come thither to see an unseeable miracle, . . . how that bread is turned into the body, and wine into the blood, of Christ, to mock our seeing, smelling, feeling, and tasting; which is a very strong faith, and more a great deal (I

think) than the text compelleth a man to. Nevertheless it were somewhat yet, if they had been as loving, kind, careful and diligent to teach the people to repent, and to believe in the blood of Christ for the forgiveness of their sins, unto the glory of the mercy of God, and of his exceeding love to us, and unto the profit of our souls; and, upon that preaching, to have ministered the sacrament as a memorial, remembrance, sign, token, earnest, the seal of an obligation, and clapping of hands together, for the assurance of the promise of God; . . .

Epistle to The Reader – 1526, New Testament (PS-1)

1.   389. I exhort thee, that thou come with a pure mind, and, as the scripture saith, with a single eye, unto the words of health and of eternal life; by the which, if we repent and believe them, we are born anew, created afresh, and enjoy the fruits of the blood of Christ: which blood crieth not for vengeance, as the blood of Abel, but hath purchased life, love, favour, grace, blessing, and whatsoever is promised in the scriptures to them that believe and obey God.

2.   390. And his Spirit shall dwell in thee, and shall be strong in thee, and the promises shall be given thee at the last (though not by and by, lest thou shouldest forget thyself and be negligent,) and all threatenings shall be forgiven thee for Christ's blood's sake, to whom commit thyself altogether, without respect either of thy good deeds, or of thy bad.

Prefaces (PS-1)
The Five Books of Moses, 1530

Genesis – 1534

1.   403. And let love interpret the law, that thou understand this to be the final end of the law, and the whole cause why the law was given; even to bring thee to the knowledge of God, how that he hath done all things for thee, that thou mightest love him again with all thine heart, and thy neighbour for his sake as thyself, and as Christ loved thee: because thy neighbour is the son of God also, and created unto his likeness as thou art, and bought with as dear blood as art thou.

2.   409. *Testament.* And circumcision representeth the promises of God to Abraham, on the one side; and that Abraham and his seed should circumcise, and cut off the lusts of their flesh, on the other side, to walk in the ways of the Lord: as baptism, which is come in the room thereof, now signifieth on the one side, how that all that repent and believe are washed in Christ's blood; and on the other side, that the same must quench and drown the lusts of the flesh, to follow the steps of Christ.

Exodus – 1534

3.   416. Now he that goeth about to quiet his conscience and to justify himself with the law, doth but heal his wounds with fretting corrosives. And he that goeth about to purchase grace with ceremonies, doth but suck the ale-pole to quench his thirst; inasmuch as the ceremonies were not given to justify the heart, but to signify the justifying and forgiveness that is in Christ's blood.

Leviticus – 1534

4.   424. So now if baptism preach me the washing in Christ's blood, so doth the Holy Ghost accompany it; and that deed of preaching through faith doth put away my sins. For the Holy Ghost is no dumb God, nor no God that goeth a mumming. If a man say of the sacrament of Christ's body and blood, that it is a sacrifice as well for the dead as for the quick, and therefore the very deed itself justifieth and putteth away sin; I answer, that a sacrifice is the slaying of the body of a beast, or a man: wherefore, if it be a sacrifice, then is Christ's body there slain, and his blood there shed; but that is not so. And therefore it is properly no sacrifice, but a sacrament, and a memorial of that everlasting sacrifice once for all, which he offered upon the cross now upon a fifteen hundred years ago; and preacheth only unto them that are alive.

5.   426. And as circumcision was a token certifying them that they were received unto the favour of God, and their sins forgiven them; even so baptism certifieth us that we are washed in the blood of Christ, and received to favour for his sake: and as circumcision signified unto them the cutting away of their own lusts, and slaying of their free-will, as they call it, to follow the will of God; even so baptism signifieth unto us repentance, and the mortifying of our unruly members and body of sin, to walk in a new life, and so forth.

6.   427. And Christ is all manner offering that is offered: he is the ox, the sheep, the goat, the kid, and lamb; he is the ox that is burnt without the host, and the scape-goat that carried all the sin of the people away into the wilderness: for as they purged the people from their worldly uncleannesses through blood of the sacrifices, even so doth Christ purge us from the uncleannesses of everlasting death with his own blood; and as their worldly sins could no otherwise be purged, than by blood of sacrifices, even so can our sins be no otherwise forgiven than through the blood of Christ. All the deeds in the world, save the blood of Christ, can purchase no forgiveness of sins: for our deeds do but help our neighbour, and mortify the flesh, and help that we sin no more: but and if we have sinned, it must be freely forgiven through the blood of Christ, or remain for ever.

Numbers – 1534

7. 429f. And so through their holy works done by the power of free-will, they excluded themselves of the holy rest of forgiveness of sins by faith in the blood of Christ.

8. 431. And yet in these works they have so great confidence, that they not only trust to be saved thereby, and to be higher in heaven than they that be saved through Christ, but also promise to all other forgiveness of their sins through the merits of the same; wherein they rest, and teach other to rest also, excluding the whole world from the rest of forgiveness of sins through faith in Christ's blood.

9. 432. For unto what further blindness could all the devils in hell bring them, than to make them believe that they were justified through their own good works? For when they once believed that they were purged from their sins, and made righteous through their own holy works, what room was there left for the righteousness that is in Christ's blood-shedding?

10. 433. We be now in the day-light, and all the secrets of God, and all his counsel and will is opened unto us; and he that was promised should come and bless us, is come already, and hath shed his blood for us, and hath blessed us with all manner blessings, and hath obtained all grace for us, and in him we have all. Wherefore God henceforth will receive no more sacrifices of beasts of us, as thou readest, Heb. x. If thou burn unto God the blood or fat of beasts, to obtain forgiveness of sins thereby, or that God should the better hear thy request, then thou dost wrong unto the blood of Christ, and Christ unto thee is dead in vain. . . . And what if thou burn frankincense unto him, what if thou burn a candle, what if thou burn thy chastity or virginity unto him for the same purpose, dost thou not like rebuke unto Christ's blood?

11. 433. Thou wilt ask me, Shall I vow nothing at all? Yes, God's commandment, which thou hast vowed in thy baptism. For what intent? Verily, for the love of Christ which hath bought thee with his blood, and made thee son and heir of God with him, that thou shouldest wait on his will and commandments, and purify thy members according to the same doctrine that hath purified thine heart: for if the knowledge of God's word hath not purified thine heart, so that thou consentest unto the law of God that it is righteous and good, and sorrowest that thy members move thee unto the contrary, so hast thou no part in Christ.

12. 436. If the priest be bought with Christ's blood, then he is Christ's servant, and not his own; and ought therefore to feed Christ's flock with Christ's doctrine, and to minister Christ's sacraments unto them purely, for very love, and not for filthy lucre's sake, or to be lord over them, as Peter teacheth, 1 Pet, v., and Paul, Acts xx.

13. 439. The purpose of thy vow must be salted also with the wisdom of God. Thou mayest not vow to be justified thereby, or to make satisfaction for thy sins, or to win heaven or a higher place; for then didst thou wrong unto the blood of Christ, and thy vow were plain idolatry and abominable in the sight of God.

Deuteronomy – 1534

14. 442. In the fifth he repeateth the ten commandments; and, that they might see a cause to do them of love, he biddeth them remember that they were bound in Egypt, and how God delivered them with a mighty hand and a stretched out arm, to serve him, and to keep his commandments: as Paul saith that we are bought with Christ's blood, and therefore are his servants, and not our own, and ought to seek his will and honour only, and to love and serve one another for his sake.

Jonas – 1534

15. 450f. Think of the law of God, how that it is altogether spiritual, and so spiritual that it is never fulfilled with deeds or works, until they flow out of thine heart, with as great love toward thine neighbour, for no deserving of his, yea, though he be thine enemy, as Christ loved thee, and died for thee, for no deserving of thine, but even when thou wast his enemy; and in the mean time, throughout all our infancy and childhood in Christ, till we be grown up into perfect men, in the full knowledge of Christ, and full love of Christ again, and of our neighbour for his sake, after the example of his love to us, remembering that the fulfilling of the law is a fast faith in Christ's blood, coupled with out profession, and submitting ourselves to do better.

16. 462. And on the other side they had set up a righteousnesss of holy works to cleanse their souls withal; as the pope sanctifieth us with holy oil, holy bread, holy salt, holy candles, holy dumb ceremonies, and holy dumb blessings, and with whatsoever holiness thou wilt, save with the holiness of God's word; which only speaketh unto the heart, and sheweth the soul his filthiness and uncleanness of sin, and leadeth her by the way of repentance unto the fountain of Christ's blood, to wash it away through faith. By the reason of which false righteousness they were disobedient unto the righteousness of God, which is the forgiveness of sin in Christ's blood, and could not believe it.

17. 463. And therefore, until that love be come, thou must knowledge unfeignedly that there is sin in the best deed thou doest; and it must earnestly grieve thine heart, and thou must wash all thy good deeds in Christ's blood, ere they can be pure, and an acceptable sacrifice unto God,

and must desire God the Father for his sake to take thy deeds a worth, and to pardon the imperfectness of them, and to give thee power to do them better, and with more fervent love.

18. 464. Which two points, that is to wit, the law spiritually interpreted, how that all is damnable sin that is not unfeigned love out of the ground and bottom of the heart, after the ensample of Christ's love to us, because we be all equally created and formed of one God our Father, and indifferently bought and redeemed with one blood of our Saviour Jesus Christ; and that the promises be given unto a repenting soul, that thirsteth and longeth after them, of the pure and fatherly mercy of God, through our faith only, without all deserving of our deeds or merits of our works, but for Christ's sake alone, and for the merits and deservings of his works, death, and passions that he suffered altogether for us, and not for himself: . . .

19. 466. And when they say that Christ hath made no satisfaction for the sin we do after our baptism; say thou with the doctrine of Paul, that in our baptism we receive the merits of Christ's death through repentance, and faith, of which two baptism is the sign: and though when we sin of frailty after our baptism, we receive the sign no more, yet we be renewed again through repentance and faith in Christ's blood; of which twain that sign of baptism, ever continued among us in baptising our young children, doth ever keep us on mind, and call us back again unto our profession, if we be gone astray, and promiseth us forgiveness. Neither can actual sin be washed away with our works, but with Christ's blood; neither can there be any other sacrifice, or satisfaction to Godward for them, save Christ's blood: forasmuch as we can do no works unto God, but receive only of his mercy with our repenting faith, through Jesus Christ our Lord and only Saviour: unto whom, and unto God our Father through him, and unto his Holy Spirit, that only purgeth, sanctifieth, and washeth us in the innocent blood of our redemption, be praise for ever. Amen.

Gospel of St. Matthew

20. 468. Here hast thou, most dear reader, the New Testament, or covenant made with us of God in Christ's blood, . . .

21. 470. All the whole law, which was given to utter our corrupt nature, is comprehended in the ten commandments. And the ten commandments are comprehended in these two, Love God and thy neighbour. And he that loveth his neighbour, in God and Christ, fulfilleth these two; and consequently the ten; and finally all the other. Now if we love our neighbours in God and Christ, that is to wit, if we be loving, kind, and merciful to them, because God hath created them unto his likeness, and Christ hath redeemed them and bought them with his blood, then may we be bold to trust in God, through Christ and his deserving, for all mercy.

For God hath promised and bound himself to us, to shew us all mercy, and to be a Father almighty to us, so that we shall not need to fear the power of all our adversaries.

22. 471. Also you see that two things are required to be in a Christian man. The first is a stedfast faith and trust in almighty God, to obtain all the mercy that he has promised us through the deserving and merits of Christ's blood only, without all respect to our own works. And the other is, that we forsake evil and turn to God, to keep his laws, and to fight against ourselves and our corrupt nature perpetually, that we may do the will of God every day better and better.

23. 474. Let us so put our trust in the mercy of God through Christ, that we know it our duty to keep the law of God, and to love our neighbours for their Father's sake which created them, and for their Lord's sake which redeemed them, and bought them so dearly with his blood. Let us walk in the fear of God, and have our eyes open unto both parts of God's covenants, being certified that none shall be partaker of the mercy save he that will fight against the flesh, to keep the law.

24. 475. And (1 Tim. I,) Paul saith, that "the love of a pure heart, and good conscience, and faith unfeigned, is the end" and fulfilling of the law. For faith unfeigned in Christ's blood causeth thee to love for Christ's sake; which love is the pure love only and the only cause of a good conscience.

25. 475. Seeing then that faith to God, and love and mercifulness to our neighbours, is all that the law requireth, therefore of necessity the law must be understood and interpreted by them: so that all inferior laws are to be kept and observed, as long as they be servants to faith and love; and then to be broken immediately, if through any occasion they hurt either the faith which we should have to God-ward in the confidence in Christ's blood, or the love which we owe to our neighbours for Christ's sake.

26. 478. And note this, that as satisfaction or amends-making is counted righteousness before the world, and a purging of sin, so that the world, when I have made a full mends, hath no further to complain; even so faith in Christ's blood is counted righteousness and a purging of all sin before God.

27. 478. Moreover, he that sinneth against his brother, sinneth also against his Father, almighty God: and as the sin committed against his brother is purged before the world with making amends or asking forgiveness, even so is the sin committed against God purged through faith in Christ's blood only. For Christ saith, (John viii.) "Except ye believe that I am he, ye shall die in your sins:" that is to say, 'If ye think that there is any other sacrifice or satisfaction to God-ward, than me, ye remain ever in sin before God, howsoever righteous ye appear before the world.'

Prologue Romans – 1534

28. 488. 'Now is the Spirit none otherwise given, than by faith only, in that we believe the promises of God' without wavering, how that God is true, and will fulfil all his good promises towards us for Christ's blood's sake, as it is plain, (chap. 1.): "I am not ashamed," saith Paul, "of Christ's glad tidings, for it is the power of God unto salvation to as many as believe;" . . .

29. 497. But as Abraham's circumcision was an outward sign, whereby he declared his righteousness which he had by faith, and his obedience and readiness unto the will of God; even so are all other good works outward signs and outward fruits of faith and of the Spirit; which justify not a man, but show that a man is justified already before God, inwardly in the heart, through faith, and through the Spirit purchased by Christ's blood.

30. 503. To abstain from adultery, as concerning the outward deed, I can do of mine own strength; but not to desire in mine heart is as impossible unto me as is to choose whether I will hunger or thirst: and yet so the law requireth. Wherefore of a man's own strength is the law never fulfilled; we must have thereunto God's favour, and his Spirit, purchased by Christ's blood.

Prologue Titus – 1534

31. 520. In the second he teacheth all degrees, old, young, men, women, masters and servants, how to behave themselves; as they which Christ hath bought with his blood, to be his proper and peculiar people, to glorify God with good works.

Prologue Hebrews – 1534

32. 523. And what is meant by that place in the tenth chapter, where he saith, "If we sin willingly after we have received the knowledge of the truth, there remaineth no more sacrifice for sin," is declared immediately after. For he maketh a comparison between Moses and Christ, saying: "If he which despised Moses' law died without mercy, how much worse punishment is he worthy of, that treadeth the Son of God under foot, and counteth the blood of the covenant, by which blood he was sanctified, as an unholy thing, and blasphemeth the Spirit of grace?"

Prologue James – 1534

33. 525. Though this epistle were refused in the old time, and denied by many to be the epistle of a very apostle, and though also it lay not the foundation of the faith of Christ, but speaketh of a general faith in God, neither preacheth his death and resurrection, either the mercy that is laid up in store for us in him, or everlasting covenant made us in his blood, which is the office and duty of every apostle, as Christ saith, John xvth.

Prologue, 1 Peter – 1534

34. 527. In the first he declareth the justifying of faith through Christ's blood, and comforteth them with the hope of the life to come; and sheweth that we have not deserved it, but that the prophets prophesied that it should be given us: and as Christ, which redeemed us out of sin and all uncleanness, is holy, so he exhorteth to lead an holy conversation; and, because we be richly bought and made heirs of a rich inheritance, to take heed that we lose it not again through our own negligence.

Prologue, 3 Epistles of John – 1534

35. 530. For he that will be justified and saved through his own works, the same doth as much as he that denied Christ to be come in flesh; seeing that Christ came only therefore in the flesh, that he should justify us, or purchase us pardon of our sins, bring us in the favour of God again, and make us heirs of eternal life with his works only, and with his blood-shedding, without and before all our works.

The Practice of Prelates (PS-2)

1. 242. [Mg.] The practice of our prelates in these days. [Txt.] Neither teach we so much as to resist your most cruel tyranny with bodily violence, save with God's word only; intending nothing but to drive you out of the temple of Christ, the hearts, consciences, and souls of men (wherein with your falsehood ye sit), and to restore again Jesus our Saviour unto his possession and inheritance bought with his blood, whence ye have driven him out with your manifold wiles and subtilty.

2. 282. When Christ, as I said, because he had no temporal kingdom, even so he meant of no temporal power, but of power to save sinners, which the process of the text declareth, by that he saith, Go ye therefore, and teach and baptize; that is, preach this power to all nations, and wash off their sins, through faith in the promises made in my blood.

3. 294. Here mark how straight the pope followed Christ's steps and his apostles! They preached forgiveness of sins to all that repented, through Christ's blood-shedding; the pope preacheth forgiveness of sins to all that will slay their brethren, bought with Christ's blood, to subdue them unto his tyranny.

4. 296. But our prelates had another secret mystery a brewing. They could not at their own lust slay the poor wretches which at that time were converted unto repentance and to the true faith, to put their trust in Christ's death and blood-shedding for the remission of their sins, by the preaching of John Wicliffe.

5. 324. The law of Moses is divided into three parts. Part of his laws are ceremonies, that is to say, signs that put men in remembrance either of the benefits of God done already, as the Easter lamb; either signs of the promise and appointment made between God and man, as circumcision; or signs that testify unto the people that the wrath of God is peaced, and their sins forgiven, as all manner sacrifices: which all ceased as soon as Christ had offered up the sacrifice of his body and blood for us; and instead of them come the open preaching of Christ, and our signs which we call sacraments.

6. 332. For it is not possible that any person baptized in the heart with repentance of evil, and with faith of forgiveness in the blood of Christ, and stedfast purpose and profession of heart to walk henceforth after the steps of Christ, in the law of God, should once desire or will to do aught openly, with long deliberation, that he would not have compared with the law of God, to see whether it were right or not.

7. 337. [Tunstal] for what service done in Christ's gospel came he to the bishoprick of London; or what such services did he therein? He burnt the New Testament, calling it *Doctrinam peregrinam,* strange learning. Yea, verily, look how strange his living, in whose blood that testament was made, was from the living of the pope; even so strange is that doctrine from the pope's law, in which only, and in the practice thereof, is Tunstal learned.

8. 343. Let us therefore each forgive other, remembering, the greater sinners the more welcome, if we repent; according to the similitude of the riotous son (Luke xv.) For Christ died for sinners, and is their Saviour, and his blood their treasure, to pay for their sins.

9. 343. These be sufficient at this time, although I could say more, and though other have deserved that I more said: yea, and I could more deeply have entered into the practice of our cardinal, but I spare for divers considerations; and namely for his sake, which never spared me, nor any faithful friend of his own, nor any that told him truth; nor spareth to persecute the blood of Christ, in as clear light as ever was, and under as subtle colour of hypocrisy as ever was any persecution since the creation of the world.

10. 344. But and if it be of a set malice against the truth, and of a grounded hate against the law of God by the reason of a full consent they have to sin, and to walk in their old ways of ignorance, whereunto (being now past all repentance) they have utterly yielded themselves, to follow with full lust, without bridle or snaffle, which is the sin against the Holy Ghost; then ye shall see, even shortly, that God shall turn the point of the sword, wherewith they now shed Christ's blood, homeward to shed their own again, after all the examples of the Bible.

Answer to Thomas More's Dialogue (PS-3)

1. 6. Take an ensample in the great commandment, "Love God with all thine heart;" the spiritual searcheth the cause, and looketh on the benefits of God, and so conceiveth love in heart. And when he is commanded to obey the powers and rulers of the world, he looketh on the benefits which God sheweth the world through them, and therefore doth it gladly. And when he is commanded to love his neighbour as himself, he searcheth that his neighbour is created of God, and bought with Christ's blood; and so forth: and therefore he loveth him out of his heart; . . .

2. 18. If a woman were driven into some island, where Christ was never preached, might she there not preach him, if she had the gift thereto? Might she not also baptize? And why might she not, by the same reason, minister the sacrament of the body and blood of Christ, and teach them how to choose officers and ministers?

3. 29. Wherefore, inasmuch as the sacraments of the old Testament have significations; and inasmuch as the sacraments of the new Testament (of which mention is made that they were delivered unto us by the very apostles, at Christ's commandment) have also significations; and inasmuch as the office of an apostle is to edify in Christ; and inasmuch as a dumb ceremony edifieth not, but hurteth altogether (for if it preach not unto me, then I cannot but put confidence therein that the deed itself justifieth me, which is the denying of Christ's blood); . . .

4. 31. And Peter answered for them all, saying, "I say that thou art Christ, the Son of the living God, that art come into this world." That is, We believe that thou art he that was promised unto Abraham, that should come, bless us, and deliver us. Howbeit, Peter yet wist not, by what means. But now it is opened throughout all the world, that, through the offering of his body and blood, that offering is a satisfaction for the sin of all that repent, and a purchasing of whatsoever they can ask, to keep them in favour; and that they sin no more.

5. 33f. Now is this a plain conclusion, that both they that trust in their own works, and they also that put confidence in their own opinions, be fallen from Christ, and err from the way of faith that is in Christ's blood, and therefore are none of Christ's church, because they be not built upon the rock of faith.

6. 35. Even so goeth it with God's elect. God chooseth them first, and they not God; as thou readest, John xv. And then he sendeth forth and calleth them, and sheweth them his good will, which he beareth unto them, and maketh them see both their own damnation in the law, and also the mercy that is laid up for them in Christ's blood, and thereto what he will have them do. And then, when we see his mercy, we love him again, and choose him, and submit ourselves unto his laws, to walk in them.

7.   40. And a thousand such superstitiousnesses setteth he before us, instead of Christ to believe in; neither Christ nor God's word, neither honourable to God nor serviceable unto our neighbour, nor profitable unto ourselves for the taming of the flesh; which all are the denying of Christ's blood.

8.   47. And when God had promised the people a Saviour, to come and bless them, and save them from their sins; the Pharisees taught to believe in holy works to be saved by, as, if they offered and gave to be prayed for: as ours, as oft as we have a promise to be forgiven at the repentance of the heart through Christ's blood-shedding, put to, 'Thou must first shrive thyself to us of every syllable, and we must lay hands on thine head, and whistle out thy sins, and enjoin thee penance to make satisfaction.

9.   56. For whosoever feeleth the just damnation of sin, and the forgiveness and mercy that is in Christ's blood for all that repent and forsake it, and come and believe in that mercy, the same only knoweth how God is to be honoured and worshipped, and can judge between true serving of God in the spirit, and false image-serving of God with works. And the same knoweth that sacraments, signs, ceremonies, and bodily things can be no service to God in his person; but memorials unto men, and a remembrance of the testament, wherewith God is served in the spirit.

10. 57. God hath created us and made us unto his own likeness; and our Saviour Christ hath bought us with his blood. And therefore we are God's possession, of duty and right; and Christ's servants only, to wait on his will and pleasure, and ought therefore to move neither hand nor foot, nor any other member, either heart or mind, otherwise than he hath appointed.

11. 57f. If I hate the law, so I break it in mine heart; and both hate and dishonour God, the maker thereof. If I beak it outwardly, then I dishonour God before the world, and the officer that ministereth it. If I hurt my neighbour, then I dishonour my neighbour and him that made him, and him also that bought him with his blood. . . . If I be not ready to help my neighbour at his need, so I take his due honour from him, and dishonour him, and him that made him, and him also that bought him with his blood, whose servant he is.

12. 58. In like manner, if the officer, abusing his power, compel the subject to do that which God forbiddeth, or to leave undone that which God commandeth, so he dishonoureth God in withdrawing his servant from him, and maketh an idol of his own lusts, in that he honoureth them above God; and he dishonoureth his brother in that he abuseth him, contrary unto the right use which God hath created him for, and Christ hath bought him for, which is to wait on God's commandments. For if the officer be otherwise minded than this, the worst of these subjects is made by the hands of him that made me, and bought with the blood of him that bought me, and therefore, my brother; and I but his servant only, to defend him, and to keep him in the honour that God and Christ hath set him, that no man dishonoureth him: he dishonoureth both God and man.

13. 59. Now let us come to the worshipping or honouring of sacraments, ceremonies, images, and relics. First, images be not God, and therefore no confidence is to be put in them. They be not made after the image of God, nor are the price of Christ's blood; but the workmanship of the craftsman, and the price of money, and therefore inferiors to man.

14. 59. Wherefore of all right man is lord over them, and the honour of them is to do man service; and man's dishonour it is to do them honourable service, as unto his better. Images then, and relics, yea, and, as Christ saith, the holy day too, are servants unto man. And therefore it followeth, that we cannot, but unto our damnation, put on a coat worth an hundred coats upon a post's back, and let the image of God and the price of Christ's blood go up and down thereby naked. For if we care more to clothe the dead image made by man, and the price of silver, than the lively image of God, and price of Christ's blood; then we dishonour the image of God, and him that made him, and the price of Christ's blood and him that bought him.

15. 59f. If (for an example) I take a piece of the cross of Christ, and make a little cross thereof, and bear it about me, to look thereon with a repenting heart at times when I am moved thereto, to put me in remembrance that the body of Christ was broken, and his blood shed thereon, for my sins; and believe stedfastly that the merciful truth of God shall forgive the sins of all that repent, for his death's sake, and never think on them more: then it serveth me, and I not it; and doth me the same service as if I read the testament in a book, or as if the preacher preached it unto me.

16. 69. Even so, not all they that were called, and also came to the marriage, which God the Father made between Christ his Son and all sinners, brought their marriage-garment with them; that is to wit, true faith, wherewith we be married unto Christ, and made his flesh and his blood, and one spirit with him, his brethren and heirs with him, and the sons of God also.

17. 70f. And they gave them significations: as holy water signified the sprinkling of Christ's blood for our redemption; which sacrament or sign, though it seem superfluous (inasmuch as the sacrament of Christ's body and blood signifieth the same daily), yet as long as the signification bode, it hurted not.

18. 73. And in like manner, because Christ had instituted the sacrament of his body and blood, to keep us in remembrance of his body-breaking and blood-shedding for our sins, therefore went they and set up this fashion of the mass, and ordained sacraments in the ornaments thereof to signify and express all the rest of his passion.

19. 76. And as soon as the signification of the ceremonies was lost, and the priests preached Christ no longer, then the common people began to wax mad and out of their minds upon the ceremonies. And that trust and confidence, which he ceremonies preached to be given unto God's word and Christ's blood, that same they turned unto the ceremony itself; as

though a man were so mad to forget that the bush at the tavern-door did signify wine to be sold within, but would believe that the bush itself would quench his thirst.

20. 81f. And we will receive of the merciful kindness of our Father; and will serve our brethren freely of very love; and will be their servants, and suffer for their sakes. And thereto, our good deeds, which we do unto our neighbour's need, spring out of our righteousness or justifying, which is the forgiveness of our sins in Christ's blood; and of other righteousness know we not before God.

21. 89. For with bodily service we can serve nothing that is a spirit. And thereto, if it were possible that all the angels of heaven could be mine enemies, yet would I hold me by the testament that my merciful and true Father hath made me in the blood of my Saviour, and so come unto all that is promised me, and Christ hath purchased for me, and give not a straw for them all.

22. 90f. And therefore we must have a rule, to know the true miracles from the false; or else it were impossible that any man should escape undeceived, and continue in the true way. And other rule than this is there not: that the true are done to provoke men to come and hearken unto God's word; and the false, to confirm doctrine that is not God's word. Now it is not God's word, if thou read all the scripture throughout, but contrary thereto, that we should put such trust and confidence in our blessed lady as we do; and clean against the testament that is in Christ's blood. Wherefore a man need not to fear to pronounce that the devil did it, to meek us withal.

23. 108f. But the preacher comforteth them, and sheweth them the testament of Christ's blood; how that for his sake all that is done is forgiven, and all their weakness shall be taken a worth, until they be stronger, only if they repent, and will submit themselves to be scholars, and learn to keep this law. And little flock receiveth this testament in his heart, and in it walketh and serveth God in the spirit.

24. 109. And if he receive any good thing of man, he thanketh God in Christ, which moved the man's heart. And his neighbour he serveth as Christ in all his need, of such things as God hath lent; because that all degrees are bought, as he is, with Christ's blood. And he will not be saved for serving his brethren; neither promiseth his brethren heaven for serving him. But heaven, justifying, forgiveness, all gifts of grace, and all that is promised them, they receive of Christ, and by his merits freely.

25. 109f. When the great multitude, that be called and not chosen, . . . that serve God night and day with bodily service and holy works, . . . behold little flock, that they come not forth in the service of God, they roar out 'Where art thou? Why cometh thou not forth and takest holy water?' 'Wherefore?' saith little flock. 'To put away thy sins.' 'Nay, brethren, God

forbid that ye should so think; Christ's blood only washeth away the sins of all that repent and believe. . . . the blessings promised unto Abraham, for all nations, are in Christ; and out of his blood we must fetch them, and his word is the bread, salt, and water of our souls.

26. 111. As when the pope saith, Ye be justified by the works of the ceremonies and sacraments, and so forth: and the scripture saith, that we be justified by the repentance of the heart, through Christ's blood.

27. 114. John i., "He gave them power to be the sons of God through believing in his name;" and John iii., "He that believeth the Son hath everlasting life;" and a thousand like texts: and another of them that be called and never elect: as the faith of Judas, of Simon Magus, of the devil, of the pope; in whose hearts the law of God is not written, as it appeareth by their works. And therefore when they believe many things of Christ, yet when they come unto the salvation that is in his blood, they be but Jews and Turks; and forsake Christ, and run unto the justifying of ceremonies with the Jews and Turks. And therefore they remain ever in sin within their hearts.

28. 114. Whereas the elect, having the law written in their breasts, and loving it in their spirits, sin there never; but without, in the flesh. Against which sin they fight continually, and minish it daily with the help of the Spirit, through prayer, fasting, and serving their neighbours lovingly with all manner service, out of the law that is written in their hearts. And their hope of forgiveness is in Christ only; through his blood and not in ceremonies.

29. 116f. If my faith be stedfast in the promises that I have in Christ's blood, I need but to pray my Father in Christ's name, and he shall send me a legion of angels to help me; so that my faith is lord over the angels, and over all creatures, to turn them unto my soul's health and my Father's honour, and may be subject unto no creature, but unto God's word in our Saviour Christ only.

30. 126. Then he bringeth in 'how the wild Irish and the Welch pray, when they go to steal;' and asketh, 'whether because they abuse prayer, we should put all praying down?' Nay, M. More, it is not like. Prayer is God's commandment; and where faith is, thee must prayer needs be, and cannot be away. Howbeit, things that are but men's traditions, and all indifferent things which we may be as well without as with, may well be put down for their dishonouring of God through the abuse. . . . And I wonder that M. More can laugh at it, and not rather weep for compassion to see the souls for which Christ shed his blood to perish. And yet I believe that your holy Church will not refuse at Easter to receive the tithes of all that such blind people rob, as well as they dispense with all false-gotten good that is brought them; and will lay the ensample of Abraham and Melchisedek for them.

31. 127. I answer, though he could prove that they prayed to saints, yet could he not prove himself thereby of the best sect; nor that it were good therefore to pray to saints. For first, the apostles, patriarchs, and prophets were sure to be followed, which prayed to none. And again, a good man might err in many things, and not be damned; so that his error were not directly against the promises that are in Christ's blood, neither that he held them maliciously: as if I believed that the souls were in heaven immediately, and that they prayed for us, as we do one for another, and did believe that they heard all that we spake or thought; . . . and though all be false, yet should I not be damned, so long as I had no obstinacy therein: for the faith that I have in Christ's blood should swallow up that error, till I were better taught.

32. 130. And as for the Turks and Saracens, that ye speak of; I answer that they were Christians once, at the leastway for the most part. And because they had no love unto the truth . . . And as for the Jews, why they bide out, is only because they have set up their own righteousness, as ye have, and therefore cannot admit the righteousness that is in Christ's blood; as ye cannot, and as ye have foresworn it.

33. 139f. I have known as holy men as might be, as the world counteth holiness, which at the hour of death had no trust in God at all, but cried, 'Cast holy water, light the holy candle,' and so forth; sore lamenting that they must die. And I have known other which were despised, as men that cared not for their divine service, which at death have fallen so flat upon the blood of Christ as is possible, and have preached unto other mightily, as it had been an apostle of our Saviour, and comforted them with comfort of the life to come, and have died so gladly, that they would have received no world's good to bide still in the flesh.

34. 142. And I feel that every soul that loveth the law, and hateth his flesh, and believeth in Christ's blood, hath his sins which he committed, and pain which he deserved, in hating the law and consenting unto his flesh, forgiven him by that faith.

35. 142f. And I feel that every soul, that beareth fruit in Christ, shall be purged of the Father to bear more fruit day by day, as it is written (John xv.), not in the pope's purgatory, where no man feeleth it, but here in this life such fruit as is unto his neighbour's profit; so that he which hath his hope in Christ purgeth himself here, as Christ is pure (I John iii.); and that ever yet the blood of Jesus only doth purge us of all our sins, for the imperfectness of our works.

36. 143. For to punish a man that has forsaken sin of his own accord, is not to purge him, but to satisfy the lust of a tyrant: neither ought it to be called purgatory, but a jail of tormenting, and a satisfactory. And when the pope saith it is done to satisfy the righteousness, as a judge, I say we that believe have no judge of him, but a Father; neither shall we come into judgement,

as Christ hath promised us, but are received under grace, mercy, and forgiveness. Shew the pope a little money, and God is so merciful that there is no purgatory. And why is not the fire out as well, if I offer for me the blood of Christ? If Christ hath deserved all for me, who gave the pope might to keep part of his deservings from me, and to buy and sell Christ's merits, and to make merchandise over us with feigned words?

37. 148f. But when he leadeth me by the darkness of sacraments without signification, I cannot but catch harm, and put my trust and confidence in that which is neither God nor his word. As for an ensample, what trust put the people in anoiling, and how they cry for it, with no other knowledge than that the oil saveth them; unto their damnation, and denying of Christ's blood!

38.   149. And when he saith, "the priest offereth, or sacrificeth Christ's body;" I answer, "Christ was offered once for all," as it is to see in the epistle to the Hebrews. As the priest slayeth Christ, breaketh his body, and sheddeth his blood, so he sacrificeth him and offereth him. Now the priest slayeth him not actually, neither scourgeth him, and so forth, throughout all his passion; but representeth his slaying, his body-breaking, and blood-shedding for my sins, and all the rest of his passion, and playeth it before mine eyes only; which signification of the mass because the people understand not, therefore they receive no forgiveness of their sins thereby; and therefore cannot but catch hurt in their souls, through a false faith, as it well appeareth how every man cometh thereto for a sundry imagination, all ignorant of the true way.

39. 149. Let no man beguile you with his juggling sophistry. Our offering of Christ is to believe in him, and to come with a repenting heart unto the remembrance of his passion; and to desire God the Father, for the breaking of Christ's body on the cross, and shedding of his blood, and for his death, and all his passions, to be merciful unto us, and to forgive us, according to his testament and promise: and so we receive forgiveness of our sins.

40. 161. First his false doctrine; wherewith the elders beguiled compel their children, and sacrifice them to burn in the pope's chastity, with no other mind than those old idolaters sacrificed their children unto the false God Moloch; so that they think by the merits of their children's burning, after the pope's false doctrine, to please God and to get heaven, clean ignorant of the testament made in Christ's blood.

41. 162f. Moreover, the priest toucheth not Christ's natural body with his hands, by your own doctrine; nor seeth it with his eyes, nor breaketh it with his fingers, nor eateth it with his mouth, nor chammeth it with his teeth, nor drinketh his blood with his lips; for Christ is impassible. But he that repenteth toward the law of God, and at the sight of the sacrament, or of the breaking, feeling, eating, chamming, or drinking, calleth to remembrance the death of Christ, his body-breaking and blood-shedding for our sins,

and all his passion; the same eateth our Saviour's body and drinketh his blood through faith only, and receiveth forgiveness of all his sins thereby, and other not.

42. 169. And when he maketh so great "difficulty and hardness in Paul's epistles;" I say, it is impossible to understand either Peter or Paul, or aught at all in the scripture, for him that denieth the justifying of faith in Christ's blood.

43. 171. Call it repentance, and then it is contrition of itself. And as for mends-making with worldly things, that do to thy brother whom thou hast offended; and unto God offer the repentance of thine heart, and the satisfaction of Christ's blood.

44. 171. Sacrament is a sign, signifying what I should do, or believe, or both; as baptism is the sign of repentance, signifying that I must repent of evil, and believe to be saved therefrom by the blood of Christ.

45. 172. As ye fashion it, mean I, and of that filthy, Priapish confession, which ye spew in the ear; wherewith ye exclude the forgiveness that is in Christ's blood, for all that repent and believe therein, and make the people believe that their sins be never forgiven until they be shriven unto the priest; . . .

46. 172. The faith of a repenting soul in Christ's blood doth justify only. And the sacrament standeth in as good stead as a lively preacher. And as the preacher justifieth me not, but my faith in the doctrine; even so the sign justifieth not, but the faith in the promise, which the sacrament signifieth and preacheth.

47. 172f. The scripture saith, that as soon as a man repenteth of evil, and believeth in Christ's blood, he obtaineth mercy immediately; because he should love God, and of that love do good works; and that he tarrieth not in sin still, till he have done good works, and then is first forgiven for the works sake, as the pope beareth his in hand, excluding the virtue of Christ's blood. For a man must be first reconciled unto God by Christ, and in God's favour, ere his works can be good and pleasant in the sight of God.

48. 178. Neverthelater, when the priest hath once rehearsed the testament of our Saviour thereon, I look not on bread and wine, but on the body of Christ broken, and blood shed for my sins; and by that faith am I saved from the damnation of my sins.

49. 178. Christ saith (John vi.), "It is the Spirit that quickeneth, the flesh profiteth nothing at all; the words that I speak," saith he, "are spirit and life:" that is, the fleshly eating and drinking of Christ's body and blood profit not, as his carnal presence profited not, by the reason of his presence only; . . .

50. 179. A perilous case. Why? Because the pope has not oiled them. Nevertheless, Christ hath anointed them with his Spirit and with his blood.

51. 179f. It is the sacrament of Christ's body and blood. And Christ calleth it the new and everlasting testament in his blood; and commanded that we should so do in remembrance of him, that his body was broken and his blood shed for our sins.

52. 183. Now answer me, by what reason canst thou make an heretic of him that concludeth nought against God, but worketh with God, and putteth that block out of the way, whereat his brother, the price of Christ's blood, stumbleth and looseth his soul?

53. 193. The Turk, the Jew, and the popish build upon free-will, and ascribe their justifying unto their works. The Turk, when he hath sinned, runneth to the purifyings, or ceremonies of Mahomet; and the Jew to the ceremonies of Moses; and the pope unto is own ceremonies, to fetch forgiveness of their sins. And the Christian goeth through repentance toward the law unto the faith that is in Christ's blood.

54. 196. Hereof ye see what faith it is that justifieth us. The faith in Christ's blood, of a repenting heart toward the law, doth justify us only; and not all manner faiths.

55. 197. And the faith wherewith a man doth miracles is another gift than the faith of a repenting heart, to be saved through Christ's blood; and the one no kin to the other, though M. More would have them so appear.

56. 197. Neither is the devil's faith, and the pope's faith (wherewith they believe there is a God, and that Christ is, and all the story of the Bible, and may yet stand with all wickedness, and full consent to evil), kin unto the faith of them that hate evil, and repent of their misdeeds, and knowledge their sins, and be fled with full hope and trust of mercy unto the blood of Christ.

57. 199f. Cyprian wrote to them, and called them the devil's martyrs, and not God's. Those martyrs had a faith without faith: for had they believed that all mercy is given for Christ's blood-shedding, they would have sent other men thither; and would have suffered their own martyrdom for love of their neighbours only, to serve them, and to testify the truth of God in our Saviour Jesus unto the world, to save at the least way some, that is to wete, the elect; for whose sake Paul suffereth all things, and not to win heaven. If I work for a worldly purpose, I get no reward in heaven: even so if I work for heaven, or an higher place in heaven, I get there no reward. But I must do my work for the love of my neighbour, because he is my brother, and the price of Christ's blood, and because Christ hath deserved it, and desireth it of me; and then my reward is great in heaven.

58. 201. And that James speaketh of another faith than at the beginning, appeareth by his ensample. The devils have faith, saith he; yea, but the devils have no faith that can repent of evil, or to believe in Christ to be

saved through him, or that can love God, and work his will of love. Now Paul speaketh of a faith that is in Christ's blood, to be saved thereby; which worketh immediately, through love of the benefit received.

59. 204. When we have sinned, we go with a repenting heart unto Christ's blood, and there wash it off through faith. And our deeds are but thanksgiving to God, to help our neighbours at their need, for which our neighbours and each of them owe us as much again at our need. So that the testament, or forgiveness of sins, is built upon faith in Christ's blood, and not on works.

60. 205f. And finally, when the peace is made between God and us, and all forgiven through faith in Christ's blood, and we begin to love the law, we were never the nearer except faith went with us, to supply out the lack of full love, in that we have promises, that that little we have is taken a worth, and accepted till more come.

61. 206. And as far forth as we have sinned, be in sin, or do sin, or shall sin, so far forth must faith in Christ's blood justify us only, and else nothing. To love is to be righteous, so far forth as thou lovest; but not to make righteous, nor to make peace. To believe in Christ's blood with a repenting heart is to make righteous, and the only making of peace and satisfaction to God-ward.

62. 207. When John said, "Behold the lamb of God that taketh away the sin of the world," he was not of that sort, nor had any sins to be taken away at any time, nor any part in Christ's blood, which died for sinners only.

Sacraments (PS-1)

1. 350. And then it followeth, that the infants that die unbaptized, of us Christians, that would baptize them at due time and teach them to believe in Christ, are in as good case as those that die baptized: for as the covenant made to the faith of Abraham went over his seed as soon as it had life, and before the sign was put on them; even so must needs the covenant, made to all that believe in Christ's blood, go over that seed as soon as it hath life in the mother's womb, before the sign be put on it. For it is the covenant only, and not the sign, that saveth us; though the sign be commanded to be put on at due time, to stir up faith of the covenant that saveth us.

2. 351. And as the circumcised in the flesh, and not in the heart, have no part in God's good promises; even so they that be baptized in the flesh, and not in heart, have no part in Christ's blood. And as the circumcised in the heart, and not in the flesh, had part in God's good promises; even so a Turk unbaptized (because he either knoweth not, that he ought to have it, or cannot for tyranny,) if he believe in Christ, and love as Christ did and taught, then hath he his part in Christ's blood.

3. 352. And likewise in their solemn feasts God commanded them to blow trumpets over the sacrifice; to be a sign unto them, that God would think on them, according to the covenant made in the blood of the sacrifice. Lo, the trumpets were commanded to be blown; not that God delighted in the noise of the trumpets, but on the faith of his people.

4. 353f. Yet in the last night, in which he had promised to smite the first-born of Egypt both of man and of beast, and to deliver them, he commanded them to take for every house a lamb or a kid, and to slay them, and to strike the door-posts with the blood, to be a sign to them, and a seal of the promise that God would deliver them that night both out of the hands of Pharao, and also from the smiting of the angel that went about all Egypt, and slew the first-born in every house. . . . In whose stead is the sacrament of the body and blood of Christ come, as baptism in the room or stead of circumcision.

5. 354. The blood stricken on the posts saved them, that they were not plagued with the Egyptians, and delivered out of the captivity of Pharao. And the blood of Christ, stricken on the posts of our consciences with a sure faith, delivereth us from the captivity of Pharao the devil, and smiting of his angels, &c.

6. 355. [Mg.] Christ's exposition of the paschal lamb. [Txt.] As who should say, 'This memorial which we yearly have hitherto observed, was once fulfilled in the kingdom of this world, when your fathers were delivered out of bondage and servitude of the Egyptians. But it hath yet another signification, hitherto unknown unto you, which must be fulfilled spiritually in the kingdom of God by my passion that is at hand, and blood that now shall shortly be shed; by the which ye shall be delivered out of the power of Satan, sin, and hell, and made heirs of the kingdom of heaven. Neither was it the lamb's blood that delivered you then (for what regard hath God in the blood of sheep and calves?) but the blood of Christ (whom that lamb figured, and described his innocence, pureness, and obedience to his Father, and compassion to mankind-ward, whose feeble nature he had put on with all the infirmities of the same, save sin) did then deliver you, to bring you to the faith of this deliverance, and to make you through faith partakers thereof.

7. 355f. [Mg.] How the paschal lamb was spiritually fulfilled in the kingdom of heaven. [Txt.] And when this Pesah was fulfilled spiritually in the kingdom of heaven by the death and blood-shedding of Christ, it ended there: and in the room thereof (concerning that spiritual signification) came the sign of the sacrament of the body and blood of our Saviour Christ, as baptism came instead of circumcision.

8. 356. (1 Cor. xi. quoted). Here ye see by these words, that it was ordained to keep the death of Christ in mind, and to testify that his body was given

and his blood shed for us. And, Luke xxii. "This is my body, that is given for you; this do in remembrance of me. And this cup is the new testament in my blood, which shall be shed for you." Lo, here ye see again that it was instituted to keep the death of Christ in mind; and to testify wherefore he died, even to save us from sin, death and hell, that we should seek none other means to be delivered with; for there is none other name for us to be saved by, but only by the name of Jesus.

9.   356f. For as the children of Israel, stung of the fiery serpents, could have none other remedy to save them from present death, than to go and behold the brazen serpent hanged up by Moses in the wilderness, which looking on only healed them; even so, if the sting of death, which is sin, have wounded the soul with the working of the law in the consciences, there is none other remedy but to run to Christ, which shed his blood, hanging upon the cross, and to his everlasting testament and merciful promise, that it was shed for us for the remission of our sins.

10. 357f. Hereof ye see also, that as the Hebrews wrote their stories in covenants and signs, giving their signs such names as could not but keep them in mind; so God the Father did follow the ensample of the people (or they following him) and commanded his promises, covenants and prophecies, to be written in gestures, signs and ceremonies, giving them names that could not but keep his covenants in mind. Even so Christ wrote the covenant of his body and blood in bread and wine; giving them that name, that ought to keep the covenant in remembrance. And hereof ye see, that our sacraments are bodies of stories only; and that there is none other virtue in them, than to testify, and exhibit to the senses and understanding, the covenants and promises made in Christ's blood. And here ye see that where the sacraments, or ceremonies, are not rightly understood, there they be clean unprofitable.

11. 358. Even so all that come to the sacrament for any other purpose than it was ordained and instituted for, that is to say, to seek absolution of their sins, with a set purpose to sin no more, as nigh as they can, and to call to memory the benefits of the passion of Christ, with the meditation to weaken the flesh, and to strength the spirit against her, and to give thanks again; that is to say, to call to mind how much he is bounden, for Christ's sake, to love his neighbour, to help his need, and to bear his infirmity and to forgive him, if he have offended and desire forgiveness, promising to amend, whereof Christ bindeth all that will be partakers of his blood; the same, I say, come thereto to their greater damnation.

12. 360. Neither is there living any man, that feeleth the virtue and power of the blood of Christ, which hath not first felt the strong pains of hell.

13. 360. And with this sacrament he (as it were) clucketh to them, as a hen doth for her chickens, to gather them under the wings of his mercy; and hath

commanded his sacrament to be had in continual use, to put them in mind of mercy laid up for them in Christ's blood, and to witness and testify it unto them, and to be the seal thereof. For the sacrament doth much more vehemently print lively the faith, and make it sink down into the heart, than do bare words only: as a man is more sure of that he heareth, seeth, feeleth, smelleth and tasteth, than that he heareth only.

14. 360. Now when the words of the testament and promises are spoken over the bread, "This is my body that shall be broken for you," "This is my blood that shall be shed for you;" they confirm the faith: but much more when the sacrament is seen with the eyes, and the bread broken, the wine poured out or looked on, and yet more when I taste it and smell it.

15. 363. "When they were eating, Jesus took bread, and gave thanks, and brake, and gave his disciples, and said, Take, eat; this is my body: and he took the cup, and thanked, and gave it to them, saying, Drink ye all of this; for this is my blood, which is of the new testament, that is shed for many for the remission of sins." First, ye see by these words, that the body was given to death, and the blood shed, for the remission of sins, and that for many. But who are these many? Verily, they that turn to God, to believe in him only, and to endeavour themselves to keep his law from henceforth. Which many yet, in respect to them that love not the law, are but very few, and even that little flock that gave themselves wholly to follow Christ. Wherefore if any man think he believe in Christ, and have not the law written in his heart, to consent that his duty is to love his brother for Christ's sake as Christ loved him, and to endeavour himself so to do, the faith of that same man is vain, and built upon sand of his own imagination, and not upon the rock of God's word; for his word, unto which he hath bound himself, is, that they only which turn to God, to keep his laws, shall have mercy for Christ's sake. "Drink of it all, for it is my blood of the new testament:" "for it is," that is to say, the drink that is in the cup, or, if ye list, the cup is "my blood of the new testament," taking the cup for the drink, by a manner of speaking used in all tongues; as when we say, 'I have drunk a cup of wine,' we take there the cup for the wine. "My blood of the new testament," that is to say, My blood, for whose shedding sake this new testament and covenant is made to you, for the forgiveness of sin.

16. 363f. Moses offered half the blood to God, and sprinkled the people with the other half, to confirm the covenant and to bind both parties: neither was there any covenant made that was not confirmed with blood, as it is rehearsed in Hebrews ix.; and as we see in the books of Moses, whose custom of blood-shedding was not only to confirm those old covenants, but also to be a prophecy of the blood that should be shed to confirm this testament. That old, cruel, and fearful testament, which drew the people away, so that they durst not abide the voice of thunder, nor the terrible sight of the fire, but went and stood afar off, was confirmed with the blood

of calves: but this new and gentle testament, which calleth again, and promiseth mercy to all that will amend, as it is a better testament, so is it confirmed with a better blood, to make men see love, to love again, and to be a greater confirmation of the love promised. For if he gave us his Son, what will he deny us? If God so loved us, when we were sinners and knew him not, that he gave his Son for us; how much more loveth he us now, when we love again, and would fain keep his commandments!

17. 364. In the old covenants the people were sprinkled with blood of calves without, in their bodies, to bind them to keep the law; else we were bound to just damnation, for the breaking of it. Here it is said, "Drink of it every one," that your souls within may be sprinkled, and washed through faith, with the blood of the Son of God for the forgiveness of sin, and to be partakers of a more easy and kind testament, under which, if you sin through fragility, you shall be warned lovingly, and received to mercy, if you will turn again and amend.

18. 365. Here is also to be noted, that the cause of the institution was to be a memorial, to testify that Christ's body was given, and his blood shed for us. And again, where Matthew and Mark said, "This is my blood in the new testament;" Luke saith, "This cup is the new testament in my blood which shall be shed for you." This is a strange speaking, and far from the use of our tongue, to call the sign and confirmation by the name of the thing that is signified and confirmed. The testament is, that Christ's blood is shed for our sins: and Christ saith, "This cup is that testament;" signifying thereby, that the thing that is meant by this ceremony is, that we believe that his blood-shedding is the remission of our sins; which is the very testament.

19. 366. For, saith Paul, "Whosoever shall eat of this bread or drink of the cup of the Lord unworthily, shall be guilty of the body and blood of the Lord:" that is to say, whoso receiveth the sacrament of the body and blood of Christ with an unclean heart, not forsaking the old lusts of the flesh, nor purposing to follow Christ, and to be to his neighbour as Christ was to him, only merciful; the same sinneth against the body and blood of Christ; in that he maketh a mock of the earnest death of Christ, and, as it is written Hebrews the tenth, "treadeth Christ under foot, and counteth the blood of the testament wherewith he was sanctified as an unholy thing, and doth dishonour to the Spirit of grace.

20. 366. Ye shall understand therefore that there is great dissension, and three opinions, about the words of Christ, where he saith, in pronouncing the testament over the bread, "This is my body;" and in pronouncing it over the wine, "This is my blood." One part say that these words, "This is my body," "This is my blood," compel us to believe, under pain of damnation, that the bread and wine are changed into the very body and blood of Christ really: as the water at Cana Galilee was turned into very wine.

21. 367. The second part saith, 'We be not bound to believe that bread and wine are changed; but only that his body and blood are there presently.'

22. 367. The third say, 'We be bound by these words only to believe that Christ's body was broken, and his blood shed for the remission of our sins; and that there is no other satisfaction for sin than the death and passion of Christ.'

23. 367. The first say these words, "This is my body," "This is my blood," compel us to believe, that things there shewed are the very body and blood of Christ really. But bread and wine, say they, cannot be Christ's natural body; therefore the bread and wine are changed, turned, altered, and transubstantiated into the very body and blood of Christ.

24. 367. The second part grant with the first, that the words compel us to believe that the things shewed in the sacrament are the very body and blood of Christ. But where the first say 'bread and wine cannot be the very body and blood of Christ,' there they vary and dissent from them, affirming that bread and wine may, and also is, Christ's body really, and very blood of Christ; and say, that 'it is as true to say that bread is Christ's body, and that wine is his blood, as it is true to say Christ being a very man is also very God.' And they say, 'As the Godhead and manhood in Christ are in such manner coupled together, that man is very God, and God very man; even so the very body and the bread are so coupled, that it is as true to say that bread is the body of Christ, and the blood so annexed there with the wine, that it is even as true to say that the wine is Christ's blood.'

25. 368f. The third sort affirm, that the words mean no more but only that we believe, by the things that are there shewed, that Christ's body was broken and his blood shed for our sins, if we will forsake our sins and turn to God to keep his law. . . . But truth it is, that the righteous liveth by his faith; ergo, to believe and trust in Christ's blood is the eating that was there meant, as the text well proveth.

26. 370. The two first parties taking the old doctors to be on their side, I answer, Many of the old doctors spake so mystically that they seem sometimes to affirm plainly that it is but bread and wine only concerning the substance, and that it is a figure of the body and blood of Christ only; and sometimes that it is his very body and blood: therefore it were needless to wade any further herein.

27. 371. And even so say they that the doctors called the sacrament the body and blood of Christ after the same manner only; because it is the memorial, the earnest, and seal of his body and blood, as the use of the scriptures is to call signs by the names of things signified thereby.

28. 372. Wherefore, seeing that all the doctors with one accord call the sacrament so earnestly a sacrifice, they cannot otherwise understand that they so say after the use of the scripture only, because it is the memorial of the sacrifice of his death and blood-shedding. Why should they then

of right be offended, if we understand the doctors after the same manner, when they call it his body and blood; and that they so call it after the use of the scripture, because that it is only a memorial of his body and blood?

29. 372. As concerning the transubstantiation: . . . Their hearts were gross, through busying themselve too much with worldly business. For the bread and wine are but only bread and wine, till the words of the testament be rehearsed over them; and then they cease to be any more bread and wine in the hearts of the true believers: for the heart, after these words once spoken, thinketh only upon the covenant made in the body and blood of Christ, and through faith eateth his body, and drinketh his blood; though the eyes, and other senses, perceive nothing but bread and wine:

30. 374. Again, seeing the faith of the testament in Christ's blood is the life of the righteous, from the beginning of the world to the end; and forasmuch as the sacrament was instituted only to bring to this life; now when they which think not the body to be present in the sacrament have by the preaching and confirmation of the sacrament obtained this life or steadfast faith in Christ's blood, . . . Faith in Christ's blood, and in the Father through him, is God's service in the spirit.

31. 374. The other part fallen therefrom through preaching the body present, serving God with bodily service, (which is idolatry, and to make God an idol or image,) in that they trust in the goodness of their works (as they which serve tyrants), and not in the goodness of God through trust in the blood of Christ.

32. 374f. Paul teacheth, (1 Cor. xiii.) that if a man had all other gifts that God can give man, and had not charity to love his neighbour, it helpeth not. For all other gifts, and the remission in Christ's blood also, are given him of God, to bring him to love his neighbour; which thing had, a man hath all; which not had, a man hath nothing.

33. 379. The words of Luke and Paul are: "This cup is the new testament made in my blood," or for my blood's sake. Now the testament is, that his blood was shed for our sins; but it is impossible that the cup or his blood should be that promise. Wherefore the sense must needs be, that it is the memorial and seal of the testament only. And therefore where Matthew and Mark say, "This cup is my blood of the new testament," the sense must needs be also, that it is the memorial and seal thereof; only calling, after the use of the Hebrews, the sign with the name of that which is signified; that is to say, calling the wine, which only signifieth the blood, with the name of the blood. And then it followeth that the bread is called his body after the same manner, because it is the sign of his body.

34. 381. Notwithstanding all these reasons, and the damnable idolatry which the papists have committed with the sacrament, yet, whether they affirm the body and blood to be present with the bread and wine, or the bread and the wine to be turned and transubstantiated into the body and blood,

I am therewith content (for unity's sake) if they will there cease, and let him be there only to testify and confirm the testament or covenant made in Christ's blood and body; for which cause only Christ instituted the sacrament.

35. 384. Wherefore, to avoid this endless brawling, which the devil no doubt hath stirred up, to turn the eyes of our souls from the everlasting covenant made us in Christ's blood and body, and to nosel us in idolatry, which is trust and confidence in false worshipping of God; and to quench first the faith to Christ-ward and then the love due to our neighbour.

36. 385. Neither ought he, that is bound under pain of damnation to love his brother as Christ loved him, to hate, to persecute, and to slay his brother for blind zeal to any opinion, that neither letteth nor hindreth to salvation that is in Christ: as they which pray to God in the sacrament not only do, but also through that opinion, as they have lost love to their neighbours, even so have they lost the true faith in the covenant made in Christ's blood and body: which covenant only is that which saveth. And to testify this, was the sacrament instituted only.

Pathway (PS-1)

1.   11. In the gospel, when we believe the promises, we receive the spirit of life; and are justified, in the blood of Christ, from all things whereof the law condemned us. And we receive love unto the law, and power to fulfil it, and grow therein daily.

2.   11f. I must therefore have always the law in my sight, that I may be meek in the spirit, and give God all the laud and praise, ascribing to him all righteousness, and to myself all unrighteousness and sin. I must also have the promises before mine eyes, that I despair not; in which promises I see the mercy, favour, and good-will of God upon me in the blood of his Son Christ, which hath made satisfaction for my unperfectness, and fulfilled for me that which I could not do.

3.   12. Nay, that is not faith, but rather a foolish blind opinion, springing of their own corrupt nature, and is not given them of the Spirit of God, but rather of the spirit of the devil, whose faith now-a-days the popish compare and make equal unto the best trust, confidence, and belief, that a repenting soul can have in the blood of our Saviour Jesus, unto their own confusion, shame, and uttering what they are within.

4.   14f. In Christ God loved us, his elect and chosen, before the world began, and reserved us unto the knowledge of his Son and of his holy gospel; and when the gospel is preached to us, openeth our hearts, and giveth us grace to believe, and putteth the Spirit of Christ in us; and we know him as our Father most merciful, and consent to the law, and love it inwardly in our heart, and desire to fulfil it, and sorrow because we cannot: which will (sin

we of frailty never so much) is sufficient, till more strength be given us; the blood of Christ hath made satisfaction for the rest; the blood of Christ hath obtained all things for us of God. Christ is our satisfaction, Redeemer, Deliverer, Saviour, from vengeance and wrath.

5. 16. The Jews seek righteousness in their ceremonies, which God gave unto them, not for to justify, but to describe and paint Christ unto them: of which Jews testifieth Paul, saying, how that they have affection to God, but not after knowledge; for they go about to stablish their own justice, and are not obedient to the justice or righteousness that cometh of God, which is the forgiveness of sin in Christ's blood unto all that repent and believe. The cause is verily, that except a man cast away his own imagination and reason, he cannot perceive God, and understand the virtue and power of the blood of Christ.

6. 17. And the poor sinner believeth, laudeth and thanketh God through Christ, and breaketh out into exceeding inward joy and gladness, for that he hath escaped so great wrath, so heavy vengeance, so fearful and so everlasting a death. And he henceforth is an hungred and athirst after more righteousness, that he might fulfil the law; and mourneth continually, commending his weakness unto God in the blood of our Saviour, Christ Jesus.

7. 18. When we hear the law truly preached, how that we ought to love and honour God with all our strength and might, from the low bottom of the heart, because he hath created us, and both heaven and earth for our sakes, and made us lord thereof; and our neighbours (yea, our enemies) as ourselves, inwardly, from the ground of the heart, because God hath made them after his likeness of his own image, and they are his sons as well as we, and Christ hath bought them with his blood, and made them heirs of everlasting life as well as us; and how we ought to do whatsoever God biddeth, and abstain from whatsoever God forbiddeth, with all love and meekness, with a fervent and burning lust from the centre of the heart.

8. 18. For it is not possible for a man, till he be born again, to think that God is righteous to make him of so poison a nature, either for his own pleasure or for the sin of another man, and to give him a law that is impossible for him to do, or to consent to; his wit, reason, and will being so fast glued, yea, nailed and chained unto the will of the devil. Neither can any creature loose the bonds, save the blood of Christ only.

9. 18f, This is the captivity and bondage, whence Christ delivered us, redeemed and loosed us. His blood, his death, his patience in suffering rebukes and wrongs, his prayers and fastings, his meekness and fulfilling of the uttermost point of the law, appeased the wrath of God; brought the favour of God to us again; obtained that God should love us first, and be our Father, and that a merciful Father, that will consider our infirmities and

weakness, and will give us his Spirit again (which was taken away in the fall of Adam) to rule, govern, and strength us, and to break the bonds of Satan, wherein we were so straight bound.

10. 19. Now Christ standeth us in double stead; and us serveth, two manner wise. First, he is our Redeemer, Deliverer, Reconciler, Mediator. Intercessor, Advocate, Attorney, Solicitor, our Hope, Comfort, Shield, Protection, Defender, Strength, Health, Satisfaction and Salvation. His blood, his death, all that he ever did, is ours. And Christ himself, with all that he is or can do, is ours. His blood-shedding, and all that he did, doth me as good service as though I myself had done it.

11. 20. Whatsoever therefore faith hath received of God through Christ's blood and deserving, that same must love shed out, every whit, and bestow it on our neighbours unto their profit, yea, and that though they be our enemies. What faith receiveth of God through Christ's blood, that we must bestow on our neighbours, though they be our enemies. By faith we receive of God, and by love we shed out again.

12. 21. If I live chaste, I do it not to obtain heaven thereby; for then should I do wrong to the blood of Christ; Christ's blood hath obtained me that; Christ's merits have made me heir thereof; he is both door and way thitherwards: . . .

13. 22. In all such tribulations a Christian man perceiveth that God is his Father, and loveth him even as he loved Christ when he shed his blood on the cross. Finally, as before, when I was bond to the devil and his will, I wrought all manner evil and wickedness, not for hell's sake, which is the reward of sin, but because I was heir of hell by birth and bondage to the devil, did I evil, (for I could none otherwise do; to do sin was my nature:) even so now, since I am coupled to God by Christ's blood, do I well, not for heaven's sake, which is yet the reward of well doing; but because I am heir of heaven by grace and Christ's purchasing, and have the Spirit of God, I do good freely, for so is my nature:

14. 23. Whatsoever is our own, is sin. Whatsoever is above that, is Christ's gift, purchase, doing and working. He bought it of his Father dearly, with his blood, yea, with his most bitter death, and gave his life for it. Whatsoever good thing is in us, that is given us freely, without our deserving or merits, for Christ's blood's sake. That we desire to follow the will of God, it is the gift of Christ's blood. That we now hate the devil's will (whereunto we were so fast locked, and could not but love it), is also the gift of Christ's blood: unto whom belongeth the praise and honour of our good deeds, and not unto us.

15. 24. These things to know: first the law; how that it is natural right, and equity; that we have but one God to put our hope and trust in, and him to love with all the heart, all the soul, and all our might and power, and neither

to move heart nor hand but at his commandment, because he hath first created us of nought, and heaven and earth for our sakes; and afterwards when we had marred ourself through sin, he forgave us, and created us again, in the blood of his beloved Son.

16. 25f. And on the other side, to know that a man ought to love his neighbour equally and fully as himself, because his neighbour (be he never so simple) is equally created of God, and as full redeemed by the blood of our Saviour Jesus Christ.

17.   26. And to know how contrary this law is unto our nature, and how it is damnation not to have this law written in our hearts, though we never commit the deeds; and how there is no other means to be saved from this damnation, than through repentance toward the law, and faith in Christ's blood; which are the very inward baptism of our souls, and the washing and the dipping of our bodies in the water is the outward sign.

Exposition of William Tracy's Testament (PS-3)

1.   274. And in the second of the first of Peter, "Which bare our sins in his body," and, "by whose stripes we are made whole." "By whom we have redemption through is blood, even the forgiveness of our sins" (Colos. I. and Ephes. I.). And, (Rom. iv.) "He was delivered for our sins, and rose again for our justifying."

2.   276. True faith in Christ giveth power to love the law of God: for it is written, (John the first,) "He gave them power to be the sons of God, in that they believe in his name." Now, to be the son of God is to love righteousness, and hate unrighteousness, and so to be like thy Father. Hast thou then no power to love the law? so hast thou no faith in Christ's blood.

3.   277. All whatsoever thou art able to do, to please God withal, is thy duty to do, though thou hadst never sinned. If it be thy duty, how can it then be the deserving of the mercy and grace that went before? Now, that mercy was the benefit of God thy Father through the deserving of the Lord Christ, which hath bought thee with the price of his blood.

4.   277f. That he excludeth, in that he saith all others be but petitioners: by which words he plainly confesseth, that other may and ought for to pray, and that we may and ought to desire other to pray for us; but meaneth that we may not put our trust and confidence in their prayer, as though they gave of themselves that which they desire for us in their petitions, and so give them the thanks, and ascribe to their merits that which is given us in the name of our master Christ, as the deservings of his blood. Christ is my Lord, and hath deserved and also obtained power, to give me all that can be desired for me; and all that other desire for me, is desired in Christ's name, and given at the merits of his blood. All the honour then, trust, confidence, and thanks, pertain to him also.

5. 278f. And as damnable as it is for the poor to trust in the riches of the richest upon earth, so damnable is it also to leave the covenant made in Christ's blood, and to trust in the saints of heaven. They that be in heaven know the elect that trust in Christ's blood, and profess the law of God, and for them only pray; and these wicked idolaters, which have no trust in the covenant of God, nor serve God in the spirit, nor in the gospel of Christ's blood, but after their blind imagination, choosing them every man a sundry saint to be their mediator, to trust to and to be saved by their merits, do the saints abhor and defy: . . .

6. 279. Yea, and I have known of simple and unlearned persons, and that of some that were great sinners, which, at the hour of death, have fallen flat on the blood of Christ, and given no room to other men's either prayers or preachings; but have as strongly trusted in Christ's blood as ever did Peter or Paul, and have thereto preached it to others, . . .

7. 280. But now, since there be more than enough, and have more than every man a sufficient living, how should he have given them, to hire their prayers, but of pure mistrust in Christ's blood? If robbing of widows' houses under pretence of long prayers be damnable (Matt. xxiii.), then is it damnable also for widows to suffer themselves to be robbed by the long pattering of hypocrites, through mistrust in Christ's blood. Yea, and is it not damnable to maintain such abomination?

8. 280. And that bestowing a great part of his goods (while he yet lived) upon the poor, to be thankful for the mercy received, without buying and selling with God; that is, without binding those poor unto any other appointed prayers than God hath bound us already, one to pray for another, one to help another, as he hath helped us; but patiently abiding for the blessings that God hath appointed unto all manner good works, trusting faithfully to his promise; thanking, as ye may see by his words, the blood of Christ for the reward promised to his works, and not the goodness of the works, as though he had done more than is duty, or all that; . . .

Bibliography

Baker, J. Wayne, *Heinrich Bullinger and the Covenant: The Other Reformed Tradition*, Ohio University Press, Athens, 1980.

Clebsch, William, *England's Earliest Protestants*, Yale, New Haven, 1964.

Foxe, John, *The Acts and Monuments of the Christian Martyrs*, ed. George Townsend, revised and corrected by Josiah Pratt, 'The Church Historians of England', George Seeley, London, 1853–1870.

Laughlin, Paul Alan, 'The Brightness of Moses' Face: Law and Gospel, Covenant and Hermeneutics in the Theology of William Tyndale', Unpublished Ph.D. dissertation, Emory University, 1975.

Luther, Martin, *Lectures on Galatians 1535, Chapters 1-4, LW-26*, ed. Jaroslav Pelikan, asst. ed. Walter A. Hanson, Concordia Publishing House, St. Louis, 1963.

Luther, Martin, *The Book of Concord*, eds. R. Kolb and T. J. Wengert, Fortress Press, Minneapolis, 2000.

Matthew, F.D., *The English Works of Wyclif*, EETS OS74, Boydell and Brewer, Woodbridge, 1998.

McGrath, A.E., *Iustitia Dei*, vol. 2, Cambridge University Press, Cambridge, 1993.

More, Thomas, *A Dialogue Concerning Heresies, CWM-6*, eds. Thomas M. C. Lawler, Germain Marc'Hadour and Richerd C. Marius, Yale University Press, New Haven, 1981.

Stibbs, A.M., *The Meaning of the Word 'Blood' in Scripture*, The Tyndale Press, London, 1954.

Trinterud, L.J., 'A Reappraisal of William Tyndale's debt to Martin Luther', *Church History*, 31 (1962), 24–43

Tyndale, William, *Doctrinal Treatises, etc.*, ed. Walter Henry, Parker Society, Cambridge, 1848.

Tyndale, William, *Expositions of Scripture and Practice of Prelates*, ed. Walter Henry, Parker Society, Cambridge, 1849.

Tyndale, William, *An Answer to Sir Thomas More's Dialogue, etc.*, Walter Henry (ed), Parker Society, Cambridge, 1850

Tyndale, William, *The First Printed English New Testament, translated by William Tyndale, 1525*, Facsimile Texts, ed. Edward Arber, London, 1871.

Werrell, Ralph S., *The Roots of William Tyndale's Theology*, James Clarke & Co., Cambridge, 2013.

Werrell, Ralph S., *The Theology of William Tyndale*, James Clarke & Co., Cambridge, 2006.

Werrell, Ralph S., 'Tyndale and the Blood of Christ', paper given at Oxford International Tyndale Conference, September, 1994.

Werrell, Ralph S., 'Tyndale's Disagreement with Luther in the Prologue to the Epistle to the Romans', *Reformation and Renaissance Review*, 7/1 (2005), 57–68.

Index